T0318212

Rhetorical Strategies for Professional Development

This book extends current research and scholarship around mentoring and learning theory, illustrating how mentoring creates, enacts, and sustains multidisciplinary learning in a variety of school, work, and community contexts. In so doing, it examines the relationship between teaching and mentoring, acknowledges the rhetorical invention of mentoring, and recognizes the intersection of gender identity (as a cultural and identity signifier or marker) and mentoring. It uses mentoring as a way to reimagine value-added approaches to research and teaching practices in rhetoric and composition.

Elizabeth J. Keller is an assistant professor of English and Linguistics, at Purdue University Fort Wayne, USA. She specializes in technical communication, workplace writing, and learning theory. Her research examines how, with the help of mentoring, people form relationships that influence their ability to write and communicate, learn, and transfer knowledge over the duration of their career. Her scholarship is available in the *Journal of Technical Writing and Communication, Communication Design Quarterly*, and *Technical Communication Quarterly*.

Routledge Research in Writing Studies

Rhetorical Strategies for Professional Development

Investment Mentoring in Classrooms and Workplaces

Elizabeth J. Keller

Routledge
Taylor & Francis Group

LONDON AND NEW YORK

First published 2019 by Routledge

2 Park Square, Milton Park, Abingdon, Oxfordshire OX14 4RN

52 Vanderbilt Avenue, New York, NY 10017

Routledge is an imprint of the Taylor & Francis Group, an informa business

First issued in paperback 2020

Library of Congress Cataloging-in-Publication Data
A catalog record has been requested for this book

ISBN: 978-0-8153-7174-8 (hbk)
ISBN: 978-0-367-60675-6 (pbk)

Typeset in Times New Roman
by Apex CoVantage, LLC

To all of the mentors in my life—thank you for showing me what I am capable of.

Contents

Acknowledgments

I want to thank my former dissertation committee who helped me plan and implement this study. Bill Hart-Davidson, Malea Powell, Dánielle DeVoss, Trixie Smith, and Michelle Eble: Thank you, thank you!

A huge thanks to the Routledge editorial staff, especially Felisa Salvago-Keyes, who helped transform this work from dissertation to book.

I'm also thankful for my research participants at Midwest Designs, HealthTech Industries, and the Residential College in the Arts and Humanities. Your mentoring experiences give me hope for new ways to mentor and teach.

To my students who have asked me tough questions and caused me to think a lot about my personal commitments to teaching, mentoring, and research: You've made me the teacher and scholar I am today.

Many thanks to Kate White, Sarah Sandman, and Suzy Rumsey. You listened to me work out complicated ideas and read drafts of chapters. Words can't fully describe how thankful I am to each of you.

I'm so thankful to have family who talked to me about things besides mentoring and supported me as I taught full time while finishing this book. Mom, Randy, and Megan: You are the best support network in the world.

Lastly, but certainly not least, Scott. Your feedback on chapter drafts, hugs when ideas were difficult for me to express, and the unconditional encouragement you gave me during this process will never be forgotten. I love you.

1 Introduction

Teaching, research, and service. The three pillars university professors are familiar with and committed to in their institutions. For nine to twelve months a year, a professor will teach several classes, contribute to the intellectual and practical rigor of their discipline, and serve on any number of department, college, university, and national or international committees. In the in-between moments of faculty life (yes, these moments do exist), something else happens:

> *The conversation after class with an undergraduate student who is interested in applying to graduate school*
> *The consolation of a graduate student who just learned they were rejected from a conference their peers would attend*
> *The coffee break with a colleague to get advice on an article that is almost-but-not-quite there*
> *The one-on-one advice from a department chair about how to craft a compelling promotion and tenure case*

Each of the above scenarios involves some kind or type of mentoring. All too often, the mentoring faculty participate in each year is viewed as an extracurricular component of the work they do. Somewhere, usually at the bottom of a CV (if included at all), is mentoring. And, more often than not, the kind of mentoring that is recorded on a CV is the kind that intersects with programmatic and systematic assessment; the kind that, for many professors and practitioners, is located when professional development activities like mentoring bleed into the required teaching, research, and service practices of a discipline. Then, and only then, is mentoring publicly visible.

Michelle Eble and Lynée Lewis Gaillet write in the introduction of *Stories of Mentoring: Theory and Praxis* that mentoring in the field of composition and rhetoric (or rhetoric and writing studies, rhetoric and writing, or writing studies) is often exemplified in the anecdotes and stories of everyday life.[1] These stories range from teacher training initiatives and programmatic and curricula development, to the delicate balances of being a parent or caregiver, while adjusting to life as a new faculty member or department administrator. Mentoring undergraduate and graduate students, junior and senior colleagues, and/or peers from other disciplines happens in a variety of ways and in various locations with material resources and technologies to help facilitate it. Simply put, mentoring relationships often happen at the same time as other teaching, research, and service responsibilities.

While mentoring in rhetoric and writing has been more significantly addressed and researched over the last twenty-five years, it is still frequently positioned as an add-on to teaching and research. Being a mentor or mentee is often considered an afterthought or undervalued task within departments and institutions, despite it taking up about as much time as teaching and research combined.[2] The reasons for this are situated in the local contexts of individual writing departments and programs; however, the ways in which mentoring is valued in rhetoric and writing practice is directly related to the ways in which teaching, research, and service are created, performed, and represented in the discipline.

The essays in *Stories of Mentoring* seek to "define the current status of mentoring" in rhetoric and writing studies by giving "insight into the character of those rare individuals who embody the term mentor."[3] The stories found in the collection are significant to particular places and time—they are situated—and they offer experiences of mentoring as students and teachers within English studies experience it. There are several sites in which to locate academic mentoring, write Eble and Lewis Gaillet, and mentoring in the field of rhetoric and composition happens most often in classrooms, faculty offices or other department spaces, and at academic conferences.[4] The professional discourses and practices that constitute mentoring are certainly diverse and are best defined in the peculiarity of everyday life.[5]

The concept of mentoring dates back to Homer's *Odyssey* and, according to Eble and Lewis Gaillet, it "signifies a range of practices and responsibilities within rhet/comp studies, but definitions of the term are hard to come by."[6] Additionally, mentoring is often a contested term, a term that concurrently "suggests identifying an earnest commitment to the development of colleagues" and students, while imposing institutional practices and disciplinary values onto those colleagues and students.[7] Such experiences of mentoring speak to, as James Inman and Donna Sewell continue, the "voice (who gets to speak as a mentor) and the authority (whose voice counts and why)" of mentoring.[8] Certainly, mentoring can be a problematic undertaking, especially for those individuals who do not benefit from particular academic investitures and practices that directly or indirectly bring about inequality instead of mutual benefit, respect, and progress.

In a field that likes to define keywords, concepts, and best practices, Eble and Lewis Gaillet further note that no extensive treatment of mentoring as an empirically studied practice currently exists.[9] They contended that much of the scholarship that existed in rhetoric and writing about mentoring did not attempt to collect and capture specific theories, histories, practices, and reflections on mentoring; rather, writing studies scholarship addressed larger topics that mentoring is certainly a part of, if only tangentially so.[10] These topics include but are not limited to the transition from graduate student to new professor, career satisfaction and advancement, promotion and tenure, and the tasks associated with writing program administration. Their edited collection began to remedy this gap in writing studies literature by highlighting selected stories from students and faculty who experienced some form of mentoring in the discipline; the essays in *Stories of Mentoring* "illustrate diverse ways in which mentoring is defined in everyday practice."[11] The collection provides "discipline-specific, candid snapshots of mentoring within the field of rhetoric and writing," which do not promote a one-size-fits-all approach to mentoring.[12]

Mentoring experiences, practices, stories, and how they function within a department or university accumulate over time, and in time, they can become the histories that shape the beliefs and attitudes of what constitutes learning. *Rhetorical Strategies for Professional Development: Investment Mentoring in Classrooms and Workplaces* takes a closer look at specific instances of how stories of mentoring accumulate in a specific context, and how those stories are arranged in relation to the beliefs, orientations, and practices of that culture. Rhetoric and writing practitioners will gain valuable insight into the complexities and capabilities of mentoring when it is used in classrooms and for career-long learning. Mentoring, as this book will show, directly informs the theories and pedagogies that constitute the field of rhetoric and composition.

Throughout the next six chapters, I will show how mentoring is a knowledge-making act, an act that is made up of a set of relational practices that are very powerful in shaping not only individual identities, but also collective workplace policies about who or what belongs in a particular place. What is more, as this book will illustrate, the act of mentoring can be a resistant one, and the participants featured in this book will illustrate that mentoring is a performance and emergence in the communities in which they belong and to which they contribute.

A Pilot Study on Mentoring, Professionalization, and Leadership

Before I begin discussing the experiences and stories of mentoring from the participants featured in this book, I first need to situate this book in a related study I conducted in the spring of 2013 with a small home construction/interior design business, Midwest Designs, located in Michigan, USA. My pilot study explored non-academic perceptions of mentoring, and how mentoring was located, named, and defined within the company. Additionally, the pilot study examined the intersections of writing, mentoring, and professionalism as experienced by the employer, employees, and interns of the company. I interviewed five people who worked for Midwest Designs: Lisa, Josh, Gabrielle, Madeline, and Jackie.[13] I interviewed them via email, and I also observed them in their work environment for one workday. I worked with Midwest Designs for two reasons:

1. mentoring is an integral part of how the company operates, and it is the foundation of the company's vision and mission statements, and
2. the owner of the company is a female entrepreneur and leader in a male-dominated industry.

The stories of mentoring that participants shared with me gave me new insight into the materialities, complexities, and possibilities of mentoring and leadership. I encouraged participants to share their experiences, stories, and memories of mentoring—I asked them to tell me their historical, cultural, personal, and professional attitudes and positionalities toward mentoring. Their stories of mentoring illustrated not only what mentoring was for them, but also how it made room for different kinds of on-the-job learning. My pilot study was guided by feminist, decolonial, and qualitative scholarship on learning, writing, and professional development, and also research on traditional, master/apprentice models of mentoring and alternative models of mentoring (i.e., co-mentoring and peer mentoring models). I learned that traditional and alternative models of mentoring could simultaneously exist, conflict, and mesh together in a particular workplace.

If theory, as Julie Cruikshank writes, is grounded in stories about everyday life, and these everyday actions, stories, and consequences produce the ways in which the past and present are thought about, then the stories participants told me about mentoring asked me to believe certain things about their workplace culture, about how mentoring is always already personal, relational, and professional.[14] The stories of mentoring that participants shared with me in this pilot study began to make visible and connect the larger ideological and socio-cultural commitments of each participant. In this way, their stories helped them translate knowing into telling, and aided in their ability to add to or challenge the conceptions of what mentoring is and how it is invented in their particular workplace culture.

When I asked one participant, Gabrielle, about the role of mentoring in the company, she responded that mentoring is more than just a feel-good after-thought. Mentoring is the everyday actions that make visible the possibilities and limits of her job along with the possibilities and limits of humanity.[15] In a similar way, another participant, Lisa, said that it is important to identify the relationship as a mentoring one because a mentoring relationship that is not clearly defined as such becomes unnecessarily complicated in terms of the roles, goals, responsibilities, and even the moral beliefs of the mentor or mentee.[16] All five Midwest Design participants agreed that transparency and reflexivity help develop and sustain a positive mentoring relationship, and when both are not present in a mentoring relationship the lack of transparency and awareness ruins the relationship, and it can cause the mentee to question the ethics and also information learned from the mentor.[17] A reflexive mentoring relationship means that both mentor and mentee are learning from each other at the same time, which indicates that a productive mentoring relationship is co-equal and reciprocal.[18] Reflexive and transparent mentoring requires mentors and mentees to ask questions of each other, and to allow for time to reflect on a completed task or goal. Employees at Midwest Designs encouraged each other to share written or other multimodal reflections on their mentoring experiences, indicating how what they learned in the relationship contributed to their professional and personal growth.

I concluded the interviews for my pilot study by asking participants a final question: *What factors affect and/or influence your relationships with the people you work with?* Participants stated that the factors that influence their workplace relationships are respect; a willingness to listen and respond to coworkers; an acute awareness of the possibilities, limitations, and interests of each relationship; collaboration; humor; flexibility; honesty; trust; and integrity. I learned from Midwest Designs that the best work environment is one that is a true democracy, a space where collaboration and equality are lived daily.[19]

I ended my time with Midwest Designs by observing employees for one 8-hour workday. I noticed where they work, how they work, and what kinds of writing and communication practices they used while working. I observed that writing played an important, even critical, part in the teaching, learning, mentoring, and business practices of the company. Participants wrote and communicated effectively by using specific writing technologies and practices, the kinds of practices that I frequently encouraged students to use in the writing courses I had taught. Because of this pilot study, my interest was piqued; could mentoring be used to help make other workplace relationships more transparent, reflexive, and productive? A year later, in my dissertation study, I would take up some of these findings in more nuanced and thoughtful ways.

A Dissertation on Mentoring, Gender, and Workplace Culture

In the spring of 2014, I began working on my dissertation study. I decided that I wanted to work with two seemingly different groups of people, so that I could explore the complexities, experiences, invention of, and stories of men and women who mentor and/or are mentored in professional (e.g., "work") spaces. I worked with employees from HealthTech Industries (Health-Tech or HTI),[20] a Midwest medical device manufacturing company, and a group of graduates from the Residential College in the Arts and Humanities (RCAH) at Michigan State University (MSU). Eight HealthTech employees were interviewed for the study, each of whom held different kinds of executive and management-level positions within the company. The HTI participants in the study were Maria, Claire, Julie, Chris, Bill, Patrick, Kevin, and Randall.[21] The three RCAH alumni who were part of this study were Alex, Carrie, and Samantha.

Participants showed me that rhetorics are multiple, motivated, actionable, and consequential. And its many networks of meaning-making exist inside and outside of the academy and are mutually constitutive of one another. Rhetorics are cultural, and cultures are persistently rhetorical; that is, meaning-making is situated in very specific cultural communities. The communities I examined in my dissertation were organized by shared beliefs and practices, and these beliefs and practices were unique to each place.

My dissertation study, from which the majority of this book draws, articulates how I conducted a rhetorical analysis of mentoring. In the chapters that follow, I explain how I, with the help of participants, located and examined the ways in which non-academic workplaces and academic cultures invent rhetorical mentoring practices. My plan was to contribute to existing scholarship and conversations about mentoring in rhetoric and writing. And as such, I developed a rhetoric or methodology of mentoring that is committed to three feminist and decolonial criteria: reciprocity, self-reflexivity (or self-awareness), and transparency.[22] This methodology can guide other professionals, researchers, and teachers in locating and inventing instances of mentoring in their workplaces and classrooms that acknowledge how a person's gender identity affects mentoring. In short, the invention of mentoring unfolds in local ways, ways responsive to local conditions of each workplace, academic space, and/or classroom.

The book's major question asks writing studies practitioners to consider how mentoring can aid in an individual's career-long, experiential learning. Several other questions inform and guide this study, and they are taken up in Chapter 2 as I begin to examine mentoring as a professional academic activity that is most visibly a part of graduate student teacher training and graduate student support. A large amount of scholarship in the social sciences and humanities concerning mentoring primarily focuses on academic perceptions of mentoring, that is, how the mentoring relationship exists in the academy, and how these relationships manifest both positively and negatively between and/or among professors and/or students. Discussions about the best practices of mentoring that occur in academic spaces are indeed useful to this study; however, the stories and experiences of HTI employees and RCAH alumni better assemble a rhetoric of mentoring that reflects the invention practices of how they mentor and/or are mentored in their workplaces. Mentoring, as a set of strategic rhetorical practices or rhetorical work, can be used to help rhetoric and writing practitioners and their students reimagine all possible knowledges and positions without reifying confining and unequal structures of power.

This book disrupts and extends current conversations within writing studies about *what* mentoring is by showing *how* rhetorical mentoring practices get invented in workplace cultures that extend beyond the classroom and other academic spaces. This rhetorical investigation and analysis of mentoring confronts and engages with ideologies and discourses of professionalism and power/authority in workplace cultures and alternative learning spaces. A participatory and inclusive process of inventing mentoring for a particular culture will be made evident in this book, as will the potential mentoring has in shifting ideas of and attitudes toward professional development and success.

Rhetorical Strategies for Professional Development takes an in-depth look at an investment approach to mentoring, which is a different kind or model of mentoring present in two different locations: HTI and the RCAH at MSU. I suggest that the kinds and strategies of mentoring predominantly used in the field of rhetoric and writing are limited in what they can do and who they can serve. As I said previously in this chapter, mentoring is often thought of as an add-on to the intellectual and pedagogical rigor that makes up academic disciplines and university departments. It is usually perceived as something peripheral yet related to how people learn. Mentoring is rarely suggested as a useful teaching tool or resource that can be used to facilitate career-long, experiential learning or different kinds of writing activities in the classroom; in fact, it is usually reserved for those students or colleagues who seek guidance and extra help because they are struggling either personally or professionally. Fortunately, this study illustrates something different—*investment mentoring*—that rhetoric and writing teachers and researchers can and should use in their practice. Investment mentoring can help undergraduate and graduate students, peer and senior colleagues, and other practitioners and professionals to be thoughtful and empathetic writers, communicators, and leaders.

In this book, I discuss how mentoring and teaching are complementary modes of learning in non-academic and academic workplaces and classrooms, and then I show how to build an investment approach to mentoring that is inclusive and equitable into rhetoric and writing teaching and research practices. Additionally, I will articulate a set of methods that can help writing studies practitioners locate and invent mentoring in their departments, programs, and classrooms. Investment mentoring, as subsequent chapters will illustrate, delineates how rhetoric and writing can shift away from master/apprentice models of mentoring and learning, and instead privilege mentoring as rhetorical work that builds productive relationships.

To reiterate, at its heart, this book is a rhetorical analysis of mentoring. Writing teachers and researchers are familiar with how to rhetorically analyze texts, images, and other print or multimedia documents and deliverables. The goal of rhetorical analysis, as all writing studies scholars and teachers know, is to illustrate how a writer writes, rather than simply stating what they wrote or created. To craft a successful rhetorical analysis, a person must demonstrate that they know how a writer used specific strategies to accomplish their purpose in writing. I approached my study of mentoring in a similar fashion. Instead of looking at only what mentoring produces (e.g., emails, memos, assessment rubrics, student papers, bottom lines, and even graduates), I looked at how mentoring was enacted in a particular workplace and academic space. I analyzed the mentoring tactics and strategies participants used to achieve their learning goals, and then I assessed some of the implications of this shift in building this kind of mentoring into classrooms, writing programs, and workplaces, both inside and outside of the academy.

My Experiences of Mentoring as an Undergraduate and Graduate Student

I tell the students I teach that my first go-around with college was anything but easy and stress-free. More than that, College 1.0 (as I call it) was downright hard for me. It was the fall of 2002, and I was attending college at a prestigious, private university dedicated to educating students in intellectually rigorous, morally, and spiritually engaged ways. I was a long way from home, and eventually I found myself struggling to keep up with and on top of assignments, lectures, exams, and other formal measures of my learning.

I received mixed messages from professors, guidance counselors, family, and friends about what I needed to do to survive in college. No matter what I did, no matter what student support services I used, or the time I spent with professors during their office hours desperately trying to catch up, the truth was that I was close to failing out of college. I searched for a mentor, for someone who could help me learn how to "do school." Despite my best efforts, I was not able to find someone to help me; in fact, I was told by a few professors that maybe I was not ready for college and that I should come up with an alternative plan for my education and career. Faced with failing grades, embarrassment, and mounting debt, I decided to leave that institution, and I transferred to a public, regional comprehensive university back in my hometown. I flourished there, not only academically, but also socially, in large part because of the mutually beneficial relationships I had with my professors and peers.

In 2011, I was admitted into the Rhetoric and Writing Ph.D. program at Michigan State University. I was seven years removed from my previous poor experiences of mentoring, and I was excited (and nervous) to be part of a challenging intellectual community. The mentoring I experienced as a Ph.D. student at Michigan State undoubtedly influenced the way I view and enact mentoring in my own teaching practices and research projects. To explain, the moments of mentoring in the Rhetoric and Writing Program at MSU happened much like the mentoring scenarios described earlier in this chapter. I have lost count of the number of times I asked my professors to help me, seeking their advice, guidance, and wisdom as I (successfully!) navigated the particular institutional structures designed to discipline me, initiate me into a new discourse community, and to help me, as David Bartholomae writes, invent the university for myself.[23] As most graduate students do, I worked hard to complete my coursework in a reasonable timeframe, and I was mentored along the way, specifically during each doctoral exam (i.e., core exam, concentration exam, and dissertation prospectus), and as I drew up the plans for my pilot and dissertation studies. I was mentored while I was "on the job market," not only by my guidance committee, but also by a group of faculty dedicated to helping those applying to and hopefully securing academic or alternative jobs upon graduation.

My reasons for writing this book are many, and they are grounded in my own experiences with and stories of mentoring. I have spent the first part of this introduction explaining what this book aims to accomplish; however, I should say something about what it is not. There are a few potential limitations to *Rhetorical Strategies for Professional Development*. The first limitation is that the relatively small number of participants with whom I worked was statistically insignificant. My study was composed of eleven participants, eight from HTI and three from RCAH. These eleven participants do not necessarily reflect every kind or type of mentoring in their specific work environments. What is more, I focus the majority of this book on what participants shared with me in their interviews. To explain, I made the decision early on in this study to focus on participants' stories and experiences of mentoring rather than the other textual documents and diagrams that I collected from them. I wanted to privilege their voices over the documents they created. Another potential limitation to this book is that, to control the temporal boundaries and scope of the study, I chose to focus this book on two key findings, despite having come up with some 200 claims about mentoring for HTI and RCAH participants. I do not, for example, devote any of the following chapters to the intersections of technology and mentoring, race and mentoring, space/place and mentoring, and age and mentoring. And lastly, I did not use all of the methods articulated in Chapter 3 with each group of participants. I used individual interviews, focus groups, and two written activities with HTI employees. I only individually interviewed RCAH students because of place and location difficulties. The study I conducted is a snapshot of mentoring for two separate groups of people, at a specific moment in time. Since I suggest that mentoring is situated and contextual, so too is this study.

Overview of *Rhetorical Strategies for Professional Development*

This book extends current scholarship around mentoring, learning theory, and gender identity performance. As such, the mentoring experiences and practices of eight executive-level employees at a Midwest medical manufacturing company are studied and analyzed alongside the mentoring experiences of three recent college graduates. The purpose of this study was twofold. First, I studied how participants enact mentoring as a mode of learning in both informal and formal ways. Second, I highlighted how a participant's gender identity greatly impacts the invention and sustainability of mentoring in their companies and classroom spaces. The findings from this study show that mentoring, like writing, helps a person convert information into useable and transferrable knowledge. Mentoring is a rhetorical skill, one that, over the course of an individual's career, acts as a powerful means to professional success. *Rhetorical Strategies for Professional Development: Investment Mentoring in Classrooms and Workplaces* is a descriptive, critical, and rhetorical analysis of mentoring for two seemingly separate yet connected audiences—executive-level managers at a Midwest medical manufacturing company and college graduates from a residential college at Michigan State University, in East Lansing, Michigan.

In Chapter 2, "Building an Investment Approach to Mentoring in Rhetoric and Writing Practice," I introduce the study's theoretical framework. I pay particular attention to how the framework described in Chapter 2 is enacted, and how it can help rhetoric and writing practitioners examine the articulation of ideologies and practices that are common in the teaching of writing and mentoring. I situate this study in three connected activities, further described in Chapter 2:

1. examining the relationship between teaching and mentoring,
2. acknowledging the rhetorical invention of mentoring, and
3. locating existing models of mentoring that are culturally and socially situated.

I frame these activities by interrogating two approaches to teaching and learning, a cultural studies approach and a decolonial one. I suggest that the heuristic proposed in Chapter 2 is one of investment and not enculturation. This unique approach to mentoring makes space for the many self-identifications of an individual who is part of the mentoring relationship.

Chapter 3, "A Feminist Methodological Approach for Locating and Inventing Mentoring," contextualizes this multisite study that was conducted in 2013–2014 by introducing two research sites: HTI and the RCAH at MSU. I begin my discussion in Chapter 3 about the HTI and RCAH participants who contributed to this study, and the unique mentoring possibilities and problems they experience every day. I analyze the methodology and methods (field observations, individual and focus group interviews, and participant-drawn mentoring networks) I describe in this chapter in relation to how I located and examined the ways mentoring functions for Health-Tech employees and RCAH alumni. What emerges is a set of practices that reveal how mentoring acts as a rhetorical tool for building and maintaining moments of experiential learning.

In Chapter 4, "Challenging Communities of Practice: How Investment Mentoring Aids Career-long Learning" I explore how mentoring operates as a mode of learning at HTI. Specifically, I outline how mentoring fits within the larger professional development goals at HealthTech, via a contextualized analysis of Jean Lave and Etienne Wenger's communities of practice and Lev Vygotsky's zone of proximal development.[24] I argue that HealthTech encourages an investment approach to mentoring (or investment mentoring), which promotes sustainable mentoring moments for employees. I end the chapter by showing the implications and risks of an investment approach to mentoring, specifically the possibilities and challenges employees face when implementing and working with and within this mentoring approach.

Chapter 5, "Investment Mentoring Is Rhetorical Work That Builds Relationships," positions mentoring as a relationship-building technique for the employees at HealthTech. In particular, I analyze how company hierarchies and employee gender identities further complicate the idea of investment mentoring explored in Chapter 4. Specifically, I suggest that mentoring, like a person's gender identity, has a performative dimension to it, and for some HTI employees, their performances of gender and mentoring are closely intertwined. Chapter 5 ends with an examination of the cost(s) of non-participation in mentoring relationships at HTI.

Chapter 6, "Pedagogical Implications for Rhetoric and Writing Studies: Case Examples of Mentoring in a Residential College," introduces, in greater detail, the final three participants in this study, three college graduates from the RCAH at MSU. This chapter extends the conversation about mentoring in non-school settings (i.e., HTI) to include the mentoring stories and experiences of RCAH alumni at MSU. Three case examples are discussed in Chapter 6, and each example from RCAH alumni paints a rich picture of the complexities, intricacies, and intersections of mentoring and learning in both school and non-school settings.

In the final chapter of *Rhetorical Strategies for Professional Development*, "Using Investment Mentoring as a Framework for Seeing and Inventing Rhetorical Work," I discuss some of the implications and recommendations of the feminist qualitative framework developed and enacted in earlier chapters of this study. Additionally, I offer suggestions to rhetoric and writing researchers and teachers that can help them facilitate hands-on, practical learning and professional identity development with their students and colleagues. To do this, I analyze the implications of investment mentoring and its impact on an individual's career-long learning trajectory. These findings are important to rhetoric and writing studies because they inform not only what can happen inside the classroom, but also what can happen in different workplaces and with different stakeholders who can influence college writing and communication. The findings from this study are considered alongside contemporary scholarship at the intersections of writing, mentoring, and distributed cognition and knowledge work. This chapter is concluded by a brief discussion focusing on future research and pedagogical interventions emerging from this study.

Initial takeaways from this study can help rhetoric and writing practitioners enact this framework in non-academic workplaces, classrooms, departments, and with colleagues and peers to help them redefine what success looks like and how it functions in our discipline. As I will discuss in Chapter 7, mentoring can be one way to perform institutional critique. In this way, mentoring can help writing studies reinterpret often-discredited service actions and practices as valuable extensions of intellectual and scholarly work. Mentoring is a micro-level action that makes visible how an institution is rhetorically constructed by human actions and interactions.

Why *Rhetorical Strategies for Professional Development*?

Although many scholars have a healthy respect for mentoring in rhetoric and writing, mentoring has not been traditionally addressed as a rhetorical skill. My study's findings show that mentoring is a critical component of a person's ability to learn, process, and retain information, and convert that information into useable and transferrable knowledge over the duration of their career. This book extends the field's current conversations around mentoring by challenging us to not only reconsider mentoring as an active component in the construction of a person's professional identity, but also to investigate how mentoring might factor into academic programs that are committed to helping students succeed in the classroom as well as the workplace. This study can act as a blueprint for other rhetoric and writing practitioners to use when researching how mentoring impacts the ways people learn and write in both university and workplace contexts.

Rhetoric and writing practitioners should enter into this book as if they are reading a study on how to find investment mentoring in their departments and classrooms, and how to create it or invent it if it does not exist. This book will also help them use investment mentoring in their own professional and personal contexts, their departments, and with their students. *Rhetorical Strategies for Professional Development* is a kind of how-to guide for locating, inventing, and sustaining investment mentoring in academic and non-academic workplaces. Writing studies should strive to have investment mentoring at the center of their vision and mission statements, at the center of departmental learning outcomes and English or writing degree requirements.

Writing teachers are particularly poised to help their students learn that if they want to write well, they have to practice investing in positive relationships with other people. Investment mentoring can help students build relationships with their peers and with their teachers. It can also act as a way to capture what is working for students in their programs and classes, what is not working, and why. What is more, the research implications for this book lie in understanding how investment mentoring can make research easier, more visible, more participatory, and more accessible to undergraduate and graduate students.[25] Investment mentoring provides researchers with a clear-cut way for working with and within cultures and communities, for prioritizing the voices of those cultures and communities without silencing them. It is a methodology that comes from cultural studies, decolonial studies, and feminist studies that keeps the researcher and their participants accountable to one another and mindful of the goals of the research process. Investment mentoring is an inclusive, checks-and-balances mentoring model. Rhetoric and writing practitioners should read this book if they want to be known as an attentive and conscientious colleague, teacher, and researcher, as someone who is considerate of and values the relationships that make work, work. Investment mentoring can make visible just how interconnected our teaching, research, and service commitments truly are.

With declining enrollments in the humanities (for any number of reasons), the field of rhetoric and writing is at a pivotal moment in its existence. It is imperative that writing studies practitioners continue to teach their students analytical reasoning, critical and deep thinking skills, and clear writing skills.[26] But more than this, we must teach students how to listen rhetorically and actively, how to be aware of and interrogate their personal, ideological, and cultural positionalities, and how to confidently challenge and disrupt the problematic systems that are, as I stated previously, designed to bring about inequality instead of reciprocity, respect, and progress. Investment mentoring can enable instances of empathetic, networked, and multidisciplinary learning; our very existence as a discipline depends on it.

I wholeheartedly believe that *Rhetorical Strategies for Professional Development* can help rhetoric and writing scholars build accountability, confidence, trustworthiness, and empowerment into the mentor/mentee relationships they have with colleagues, students, and community members.[27] In turn, students will graduate from our programs and departments equipped with the skills necessary to be loyal and invested, and encouraging colleagues in whatever line of work they pursue.

Notes

1. Michelle F. Eble and Lynée Lewis Gaillet, *Stories of Mentoring: Theory and Praxis* (West Lafayette: Parlor Press, 2008), 3.
2. Theresa Enos, *Gender Roles and Faculty Lives in Rhetoric and Composition* (Carbondale: SIU Press, 1996); Rebecca Rickly and Susanmarie Harrington, "Feminist Approaches to Mentoring Teaching Assistants: Conflict, Power, and Collaboration," in *Preparing College Teachers of Writing: Histories, Theories, Programs, and Practices*, eds. Betty Pytlik and Sarah Liggett (New York: Oxford University Press, 2002); Sally Barr Ebest, "Mentoring: Past, Present, and Future," in *Preparing College Teachers of Writing: Histories, Theories, Programs, and Practices*, eds. Betty Pytlik and Sarah Liggett (New York: Oxford University Press, 2002); Pamela VanHaitsma and Steph Ceraso, "'Making It' in the Academy through Horizontal Mentoring," *Peitho* 19, no. 2 (2017).
3. Eble and Lewis Gaillet, *Stories*, 3.
4. Eble and Lewis Gaillet, *Stories*, 5–6.
5. Michel de Certeau, *The Practice of Everyday Life* (Berkeley: University of California Press, 1984); Carl Herndl, "Teaching Discourse and Reproducing Culture: A Critique of Research and Pedagogy in Professional and Non-academic Writing," *College Composition and Communication* 44 (1993).
6. Eble and Lewis Gaillet, *Stories*, 4.
7. James Inman and Donna Sewell, "Mentoring in Electronic Spaces: Using Resources to Sustain Relationships," in *The Center Will Hold*, ed. Michael Pemberton (Logan: Utah State University, 2003), 179.
8. Inman and Sewell, "Mentoring," 179.
9. Eble and Lewis Gaillet, *Stories*, 7.
10. Eble and Lewis Gaillet, *Stories*, 5–7.
11. Eble and Lewis Gaillet, *Stories*, 11.
12. Eble and Lewis Gaillet, *Stories*, 11.
13. Participant names have been changed to protect their identities.

14. Julie Cruikshank, *The Social Life of Stories: Narrative and Knowledge in the Yukon Territory* (Lincoln: University of Nebraska Press, 2000), 3, 11.
15. Gabrielle, email response to the author, January 2013.
16. Lisa, email response to the author, January 2013.
17. Gabrielle, email response to the author, January 2013.
18. Jackie, email response to the author, January 2013.
19. Gabrielle, email response to the author, January 2013.
20. Company name has been changed to protect employees' identities.
21. Participant names have been changed to protect their identities.
22. Patti Lather, "Research as Praxis," *Harvard Educational Review* 56, no. 3 (September 1986); Gloria Anzaldúa, *Borderlands/La Frontera: The New Mestiza* (San Francisco: Aunt Lute Books, 1987); Linda Tuhiwai Smith, *Decolonizing Methodologies: Research and Indigenous Peoples* (London: Zed Books, 1999); Walter Mignolo, *The Darker Side of Western Modernity: Global Futures, Decolonial Options* (Durham: Duke University Press Books, 2011); and Malea Powell, "Dreaming Charles Eastman: Cultural Memory, Autobiography, and Geography in Indigenous Histories," in *Beyond the Archives: Research as a Lived Process*, eds. Gesa Kirsch and Liz Rohan (Carbondale: Southern Illinois University Press, 2008).
23. David Bartholomae, "Inventing the University," *The Journal of Basic Writing* 5, no. 1 (1986).
24. Jean Lave and Etienne Wenger, *Situated Learning: Legitimate Peripheral Participation* (Cambridge: Cambridge University Press, 1991); Lev Vygotsky, *Mind in Society: The Development of Higher Psychological Processes* (Cambridge, MA: Harvard University Press, 1978).
25. Patricia Sullivan, Michele Simmons, Kristen Moore, Lisa Meloncon, and Liza Potts, "Intentionally Recursive: A Participatory Model for Mentoring," *Proceedings of the 33rd Annual International Conference on the Design of Communication* (July 2015); Heather Noel Turner, Minh-Tam Nguyen, Beth Keller, Donnie Johnson Sackey, Jim Ridolfo, Stacey Pigg, Benjamin Lauren, Liza Potts, Bill Hart-Davidson, and Jeff Grabill, "WIDE Research Center as Incubator for Graduate Student Experience," *Journal of Technical Writing and Communication* 47, no. 2 (March 2017).
26. Heidi Tworek, "The Real Reason the Humanities are 'in Crisis'," *The Atlantic*, www.theatlantic.com/education/archive/2013/12/the-real-reason-the-humanities-are-in-crisis/282441/; Colleen Flaherty, "Major Exodus," *Inside Higher Ed*, www.insidehighered.com/news/2015/01/26/where-have-all-english-majors-gone.
27. Karen Keller, *Influence: What's the Missing Piece* (Dallas: Executive Press, Inc., 2017).

2 Building an Investment Approach to Mentoring in Rhetoric and Writing Practice

> Narrative might well be considered a solution to a problem of general human concern, namely, the problem of how to translate knowing into telling.
> —Hayden White, *The Content of the Form: Narrative Discourse and Historical Representation*

This chapter assembles a methodology for rhetoric and writing practitioners to use in locating and inventing an investment approach to mentoring in their departments, programs, and classrooms. Throughout this book, I use the word *invention* in its most literal sense; according to *Merriam-Webster's*, to invent something means to create, develop, or design a thing, process, or practice.[1] I also pay special attention to the individual, social, and contextual motivations for invention to occur.

Additionally, I use the word *investment* in two ways throughout this book:

1. from the late fifteenth century meaning to indicate the act of putting on vestments, or to dress oneself, and
2. from the contemporary meaning to contribute to, especially in terms of human, social, or financial capital.[2]

For the purposes of this chapter, investment means *to figuratively clothe oneself as a professional by self-selecting professional development practices that best suit their needs, much like a person would select what they wear each day*. It should be noted, too, that HealthTech Industries (HTI) employees and the Residential College in the Arts and Humanities (RCAH) alumni used this contemporary meaning of investment to describe the mentoring opportunities available to them at work and school. Their stories of mentoring are the groundwork for this study that makes it possible to locate, invent, and sustain fair and equitable mentoring practices.

The definition of feminism I use throughout this chapter and book draws from Jacqueline Jones Royster's and Gesa Kirsch's work on how feminist rhetorical practices are changing the ways research is done and valued in rhetoric and writing studies.[3] They write that feminism is the "commitment to justice, equality, empowerment, and peace, while keeping the contours of this notion dynamic and open, resisting the deep desire to speak as if there is no need for negotiation."[4] This explanation of feminism is broad enough to locate all kinds and types of mentoring, and also offers boundaries that are "open and dynamic" to underrepresented or non-traditional experiences of mentoring. The invention of sustainable and equitable mentoring practices in a department, classroom, or workplace is committed to three feminist and decolonial criteria:

1. reciprocity,
2. self-reflexivity (or self-awareness), and
3. transparency.[5]

In short, an investment approach to mentoring is a necessary component of individual, career-long, and programmatic development.

The foundation for understanding mentoring as rhetorical work is built by drawing most heavily from contemporary rhetoric and writing, cultural and feminist studies, and technical communication scholarship. This scholarship best describes how mentoring and mentoring in the workplace is or is not engaged. Additionally, I use scholarship from outside of rhetoric and writing studies to further situate participants' experiences in the following chapters, to more fully leverage important details that may be missed at first glance. To this end, three sets of questions guide this study and reflect the personal, relational, and professional nature of mentoring:

1. *Do workplace cultures invent mentoring practices? If so, how? How is the invention of mentoring in a workplace negotiated in relation to one's sex and/or gender identity?*

For the employees at HTI and RCAH alumni, mentoring practices are invented and re-invented daily. This invention and re-invention of mentoring prioritizes an individual's ability to self-identify and self-develop as a skilled expert in their workplace. Specifically in Chapter 5, HTI employees share how their gender identity is connected to and deeply informs their past, present, and future mentoring practices while at work.

2. *Are there connections between or among reciprocity, self-reflexivity (or self-awareness), and transparency, and the invention of mentoring practices in a workplace? What might this mean for career-long learning?*

These three criteria (reciprocity, self-reflexivity, and transparency) can either make or break a mentoring relationship. A mutually beneficial mentoring relationship is invented when the individuals involved in the mentoring relationship embrace reciprocity, self-reflexivity (or self-awareness), and transparency. In Chapter 4, I show that to invent sustainable and fair mentoring practices requires individual and collective growth, and clear, direct, and honest communication. This approach to mentoring is one of investment instead of enculturation.

3. *What are the possibilities for understanding mentoring as rhetorical work? How can mentoring be used as a heuristic or template for an individual's professional identity development?*

Mentoring is rhetorical work, and as the experiences of HTI employees and RCAH alumni illustrate, the kind of work that aids in an individual's career-long, experiential learning. Investment mentoring can help an individual develop their professional identity without dismissing or covering up their gender identity.

I answer the questions posed above in more detail throughout this book, and I provide insights that guide programmatic and pedagogical decisions regarding the preparation of students as successful writers and communicators. In Chapters 4, 5, and 6 the mentoring practices of eleven participants, eight employees from HTI and three alumni from RCAH, are explored to show the connection between mentoring in school and non-school settings. This study shows how a participant's mentoring experiences can indicate and even predict the kind and level of value added to their work/professional and home/personal lives.

What emerges from participants' stories is a methodology grounded in feminist, decolonial, and qualitative theory and practice, a methodology for locating, examining, and inventing value in rhetoric and writing practice through an investment approach to mentoring. The idea of mentoring as rhetorical work can help practitioners better identify, assess, appreciate, and encourage the connections between rhetoric and writing programs and industry work, and how teachers can best prepare their students for career-long, experiential learning.

In the following sections, I introduce and situate a heuristic for professional identity development that works through the following three connected activities:

1. examining the relationship between teaching and mentoring,
2. acknowledging the rhetorical invention of mentoring, and
3. locating existing models of mentoring that are culturally and socially situated.

These activities can build a framework for seeing and inventing value-added approaches to research and teaching practices in rhetoric and writing studies. Put another way, they extend contemporary writing studies scholarship and recent conversations surrounding value or value-added approaches to teaching and research in writing studies, by reflecting on how mentoring can build long-lasting and impartial value in writing studies programs.[6]

The Relationship between Teaching and Mentoring in Rhetoric and Writing

Teaching and mentoring are complementary modes of learning. In order for me to explain how mentoring can build value in writing studies, I must discuss approaches to teaching that account for the cultural identifications of students and teaching practices. To begin, much of the scholarship that is focused on the intersections of workplace writing and learning on-the-job is associated with professional writing and technical communication. Writing and communicating in professional environments (e.g., workplaces) often require an individual to use specialized language while simultaneously working with and for multiple and different audiences. And, as Bernadette Longo points out, workplace writing is often taken up in two ways:

1. As an object of study, and
2. As a process that visibilizes the structures of colonization still in place in various professions and workplaces.[7]

Longo describes a cultural study of technical communication and workplace writing that focuses on five themes:

1. the object as discourse,
2. the object within cultural context,
3. the object within historical context,
4. the object as ordered, and
5. the relationship of the object with the one who studies it.[8]

With Longo's five themes in mind, two significant approaches to teaching in rhetoric and writing are extended to mentoring: a cultural studies approach and a decolonial approach. Later in this chapter and in Chapter 3, I explain a combination of these approaches as a methodology for inventing and examining mentoring in classrooms and workplaces. Extending these teaching approaches to how mentoring happens can give rhetoric and writing practitioners a better idea how institutions organize and discipline the people who make up those institutions. While a cultural studies approach to research and teaching in rhetoric and writing can be a useful and is a much used through-point for teaching writing, a decolonial approach to research, teaching, and mentoring in rhetoric and writing enables writing researchers and teachers to, as Angela Haas writes "interrogate the colonial powers and discourses still at play in the ways we continue to make sense of the world."[9]

In the 1960s, an academic field emerged at the intersections of critical theory and literary criticism. This new approach to understanding everyday lives—cultural studies or cultural theory—closely examines the things, objects, and messages that are related to ideologies, discourses, and conflicts associated with race, social class, gender, and other identity positions. According to cultural studies theorist Stuart Hall, the production of an individual's cultural identity is never complete and always in process; the articulations of an individual's identity are always contingent and are always possible.[10] Cultural identity permits an individual to "see and recognize the different parts and histories of ourselves, to construct those points of identification, those positionalities," and ultimately participate in the construction of individual and collective identities.[11] An individual's identity development, he explains, is continuous and ongoing and therefore situated among the many categories of self they claim—it is the actual linkage of rhetorical practice or articulation to identity construction. Hall situates the composition of cultural identity further, writing,

> It is a matter of "becoming" as well as of "being," where . . . cultural identities come from somewhere, have histories, . . . undergo constant transformation, . . . and are subject to the continuous "play" of history, culture, and power.[12]

An individual's identity is not fixed or tied to a specific location or time, but rather is informed by past, current, and future experiences that are socially and communally created. An individual's identity is unstable, decentered, permeable, and constituted by the multitude of ways they are positioned by and within narratives of history and culture. A cultural studies approach to research and teaching writing seeks to understand "the relationship between these culturally saturated local knowledges and practices, and economics, politics, hegemony, and agency."[13] Similarly, a cultural studies approach to understanding mentoring requires rhetoric and writing practitioners to "address relationships between and among power and knowledge, multiculturalism, postmodernism, gender, conflict and ethics."[14] To do anything less would be irresponsible.

Carolyn Miller offers humanistic connections between what writing is and what its role is in communicative practice.[15] She urges writing teachers and researchers to improve the teaching and study of writing by reevaluating reliance on positivist views of science and rhetoric. The positivist view of science, and by extension scientific, technical, and workplace rhetoric, positions communication and writing as skills of "subduing language" so that language might efficiently and deliberately force minds into a particular kind of reality.[16] A positivist approach to research and teaching in writing studies prioritizes reporting information efficiently, accurately, and objectively, and often at the expense of human emotion.[17] So, to combat this problematic view of writing and communication, Miller suggests that a "humanistic rationale" for rhetoric and writing practice is needed, where,

> To write, to engage in any communication, is to participate in a community; to write well is to understand the conditions of one's own participation—the concepts, values, traditions, and style which permit identification with that community and determine the success or failure of communication.[18]

In other words, rhetoric and writing researchers and teachers must convey to students that writers and communicators are not merely interpreters of unfamiliar concepts or specialized writing, but rather participants in open, dynamic, and shifting communication systems. Researchers, teachers, and students are all participants in shifting systems of power, communication, and knowledge production. It is in these moments of shift or change that the significance of relationship building is most visible. If writing teachers and researchers are seriously invested in teaching students how to write well, then they must have the necessary tools, resources, and space to develop humanistic and culturally aware relationships with one another. The communities in which they belong and work depend on it.

Another concern for rhetoric and writing practitioners is how they address the relationship among ideological and cultural production, discourse, and teaching in their classroom and workplaces. Carl Herndl writes that if writing teachers are uncritical in research and teaching "[students will not] perceive the cultural consequences of a dominant discourse or the alternate understandings it excludes."[19] For Miller and Herndl, rhetoric and writing teachers and students must take responsibility for their beliefs and actions, and must understand those beliefs and actions as ideologically and culturally situated. An investment approach to mentoring can help teachers and students to be accountable to the writing they produce and the decisions and actions of which their writing guides.

Many writing studies teachers and researchers have abandoned the current-traditional notion of writing practice as an indifferent, apolitical skill; however, some teachers and researchers still today have not. To do so, they must, according to Herndl, "recognize that discourse is inseparable from institutions, from organizational structures, from disciplinary and professional knowledge claims and interests, and from the day-to-day interaction of workers."[20] Rhetoric and writing teachers are "unavoidably engaged in the production of professional and cultural power," through the very traditional pedagogies and methods they use in the classroom, where it can be easy and convenient to overlook contesting positions and, ultimately, cultures.[21] Therefore, resistance becomes an essential component for a writing pedagogy aimed at political and cultural self-consciousness and liberation.[22] Mentoring, as a set of strategic rhetorical practices or rhetorical work, can be used to help rhetoric and writing practitioners and students reimagine all possible knowledges and positions without reifying confining and unequal structures of power. Again, writing teachers doing anything less would be careless and irresponsible.

As I previously mentioned in this chapter, Longo and other rhetoric and writing scholars advocate for a "cultural turn" that seeks to make more visible the struggles for legitimating knowledge production in rhetoric and writing practice.[23] This "cultural turn" as Scott and Longo note, is "a narrow contextual focus on discrete organizational discourse communities, [a] mostly explanatory and pragmatic stance, and [an] elision of the politics of knowledge legitimation."[24] Scott and Longo use Michel Foucault's *The Archaeology of Knowledge* to understand how discourses participate in power/knowledge systems, which inform writing research and teaching.[25] Foucault writes that the task of discourse is to make differences—to constitute those differences as objects, to analyze them, and to define their concept.[26] Mentoring is a tactic that can be used to "reveal discursive practices in their complexity and density; to show that to speak is to do something—something other than to express what one thinks," namely to construct, legitimize, or dismantle knowledge.[27] A cultural studies approach to writing studies practice "can illuminate how the struggles for knowledge legitimation that take place within [writing] practices are influenced by institutional, political, economic, and/or social relationships and tensions."[28] Similarly, investment mentoring can, at the very least, make visible the social relationships and tensions that control knowledge production. An investment approach to mentoring facilitates discussions of power, politics, and other cultural tensions. Investment mentoring can further expose the complexities associated with writing and the teaching of writing.

A cultural studies approach to research and teaching in writing studies makes space for otherwise invisible intricacies found within writing and writing instruction. These complexities include but are not limited to the ways in which writing and the teaching of writing can simultaneously legitimate certain knowledges, discourses, cultures, and individuals, and subjugate others. A cultural studies approach to research, teaching, and mentoring can critique instances of writing that attempt to control and speak for others. Still, a cultural studies approach to mentoring falls short in equipping practitioners with ways to move beyond critique, to interrogate their own and others' positions in relation to systems of power. A cultural studies approach to mentoring in rhetoric and writing is a useful place to start. However, a decolonial approach to research, teaching, and mentoring in rhetoric and writing provides a better way to orient the commitments and practices teachers value when the teaching of writing is discussed.

Several scholars promote a decolonial approach to research and teaching in higher education.[29] A decolonial approach to learning, research, and teaching can guide people who are interested in locating and inventing mentoring in their workplace. This way of mentoring calls upon contemporary decolonial scholars to illuminate how a decolonial approach to teaching and research in rhetoric and writing can be applied to mentoring.[30] Unlike a cultural studies approach to mentoring, a decolonial approach to understanding writing and mentoring insists that an individual actively resist power and control by confronting and delinking from hegemonic and colonial institutional practices.

To better understand how people resist structures of power and control, Michel de Certeau's work on the practices of everyday life is particularly useful.[31] He analyzes a plurality of everyday, individual relationships, where these relationships make up culture or are understood as "systems of operational combination."[32] Everyday practices are, according to de Certeau, "ways of operating" like walking, reading, producing, and speaking.[33] He asserts that everyday practices should not be understood as merely the background of social life, but should instead explain mass cultural productions. These cultural productions, for instance, present how professional documents and workplace relationships and ideologies are produced and reproduced.

Everyday practices can subvert institutions of control and power. This is accomplished through actions called tactics. A tactic is "a calculated action determined by the absence of a proper locus. The space of a tactic is the space of the other."[34] Ordinary, and often marginalized, people use tactics to alter the production of objects, traditions, and ways of knowing or being in relation to laws, language, and otherwise acceptable ways of production. Laws and languages are manifestations of power relationships or strategies. A strategy, writes de Certeau, is "the calculation (or manipulation) of power relationships that becomes possible as soon as a subject with will and power (a business, an army, a city, a scientific institution) can be isolated."[35] This reappropriation of what constitutes culture allows people to challenge and destabilize the beliefs that make up institutions that impose correct or legitimated ways of knowing and doing on them. Everyday practices must be prioritized in rhetoric and writing practice because everyday practices constitute how all texts and all cultures are created, privileged, or ignored.

A tactical or decolonial approach to learning, research, and teaching affords individuals the chance to locate and explore their everyday practices and how those practices contribute to or challenge the top-down or bottom-up structures of knowledge and discipline.[36] De Certeau points out that cultures are practiced into life every day; they do not occur randomly or without context. And, while not every action is in relation to an overt system of power, writing and mentoring are embedded in cultural practices that get made and remade every time something is written, communicated, and/or performed. Practices, tactics, and strategies help locate spaces of intervention within discourses of disciplinary, institutional, and professional power. Mentoring, when thought of as a tactic, is not only a process of cultural study that can influence the texts, relationships, and cultures it produces, but also a set of practices that encourage rhetorical invention and intervention.

Linda Tuhiwai Smith proposes a methodology that seeks to undo the web of imperialism and colonialism of indigenous peoples.[37] She notes that the past and present, local and global communities, languages, and social practices are "spaces of marginalization [and] also spaces of resistance and hope."[38] Her methodology is a "framework of self-determination, decolonization, and social justice."[39] Although Tuhiwai Smith offers a decolonizing methodology for the Maori of New Zealand, her work influences a decolonial approach to teaching, research, and learning in rhetoric and writing studies. To explain, decolonial tactics can help writing students and teachers gain a "critical understanding of the underlying assumptions, motivations, and values which inform research practices," and other everyday and workplace practices as well.[40] Investment mentoring, which is grounded in feminist, cultural, and decolonial approaches to teaching and learning, can lead to moments of discovery and rediscovery, of claiming and reclaiming the self.

A decolonial approach to learning in writing studies assists teachers in exposing how certain writing practices can serve cultural and even technological hegemony; a decolonial approach advocates resistance of those imbalances of power. Mentoring, like research and teaching, can structure meaning-making systems and the practices and bodies associated with and within those systems in ways that are more equitable. A decolonial mentoring network can present individuals with the intellectual tools to make visible the structures of colonization in cultural and textual production, to assess their position within those structures, and to not be shamed into silence upon their findings. Mentoring, as a set of rhetorical practices or rhetorical work, is a web of relations that can reveal oppressive and hidden knowledge-making systems found within many professional discourses and contemporary workspaces.

A decolonial and critical race studies' approach to technical and professional writing research and teaching also informs an investment approach to mentoring.[41] Specifically, as Angela Haas writes, it is crucial for writing studies to understand "how race and place matter to technical communication research, scholarship, curriculum design, and pedagogy."[42] She challenges writing practitioners to consider how language might serve to reconstitute "the long standing legacies of colonialism and imperialism, particularly in the rhetoric that we choose to employ to represent our work and the work of others."[43] Despite the amount of historical and contemporary scholarship concerned with the cultural influences and effects of writing practices, Haas points out that Scott and Longo explicitly made the case for rhetoric and writing research that is grounded in cultural studies and not merely paid lip service.[44] And, although Scott and Longo explicitly called for scholarship grounded in cultural studies, Haas argues that technical and professional writing has a history of ignoring "the ways in which our work is saturated with white male culture—which has real effects related to privilege and oppression on the lives and work of designers, writers, editors, and audiences of technical communication."[45] Investment mentoring is one way teachers and researchers can examine and own up to the kinds of potentially exclusive practices that constitute research, pedagogy, and what counts as success in rhetoric and writing.

Writing practices are continuously cultural. And mentoring that is coupled with decolonial options for rhetoric and writing practice can enable practitioners to reimagine and reconstruct the recognition and negotiation of cultural information to spur on social action. Writing studies teachers and researchers have the responsibility—the obligation—to use mentoring in classrooms and other learning spaces to make room for responsible discourse. A decolonial approach to research, teaching, and learning supports the interconnectedness of bodies and things, a kind of bridge connecting cultural studies options with decolonial ones. For Haas, decolonial methodologies and pedagogies serve two purposes,

> To redress colonial influences on perceptions of people, literacy, language, culture, and community and the relationships therein and support the coexistence of cultures, languages, literacies, memories, histories, places, and spaces—and encourage respectful and reciprocal dialogue between and across them.[46]

Thus, cultural studies options for research and teaching combined with decolonial options is what is referred to in Chapter 3 as a feminist, qualitative, and rhetorical methodology for locating and inventing mentoring in school and non-school settings. This methodology for studying and inventing mentoring in rhetoric and writing studies insists upon teachers and researchers to provide students with non-oppressive options for rethinking and reorganizing their narratives of work, school, and other learning and writing practices. The overall goal of this book is to help teachers, researchers, and students locate and invent investment mentoring, which is both equitable and sustainable.

The Rhetorical Invention of Mentoring

So, what do I mean when I use the word mentoring in this study? According to *Merriam-Webster's*, the word mentor dates to 1616, and is defined as "a trusted counselor or guide; a coach, counsel, guide, or tutor."[47] This definition provides a starting point in understanding who a mentor is and the qualities a good mentor possesses. Rhetoric and writing practitioners use the word mentor (or mentoring, mentorship, mentoring relationship, and mentoring network) to encompass a relationship or network consisting of two or more people with the purpose of helping the individuals involved grow intellectually, socially, and professionally.[48] While mentoring shifts based on context (e.g., geographical location or physical space) and available resources, this shift also occurs because of the individual needs of the mentor and mentee. For example, an individual (mentee) might seek the guidance of a more experienced colleague (mentor) to help them secure a promotion at work. If the mentee receives the promotion, it is inferred that they no longer need the support of their mentor for this task, and therefore the relationship shifts to a new professional goal, or it ends. With that said, writing researchers and teachers often use the dictionary definition of mentoring as an entry point in much of the current scholarship, teaching practices, and informal conversations surrounding mentoring.[49]

To illustrate more specifically, Jennifer Clary-Lemon and Duane Roen write that networks of mentoring are multiple, and that a single network or relationship may nurture and shelter and also isolate and alienate mentees and mentors from scholarly and social efficiency.[50] Mentoring should be located "as a scholarly practice," contend Clary-Lemon and Roen, and that a lack of critical definition of mentoring can lead to it being invisible, undervalued, or not valued at all.[51] Further, mentoring is "somewhere between service and teaching," notes Cindy Moore, and that mentoring becomes easily dismissed because of its often invisible and somewhat in-between feel.[52] Moore carefully articulates how tricky it is to locate the personal in professional spaces; she writes that some faculty avoid mentoring altogether for a variety of reasons, including the blurred personal and collaborative nature of mentoring, which can leave both mentor and mentee feeling vulnerable.[53] Mentoring, and the ways it is enacted in academic and other professional settings, must be understood in relation to and informed by ideological, political, and other social commitments.

In a similar way, rhetoric and writing studies must, according to Wendy Sharer, Jessica Enoch, and Cheryl Glenn, expand current conversations that connect professionalism to mentoring beyond teacher training.[54] Instead, the connection between professionalism and mentoring must include "mentoring necessary for becoming a well-rounded professional, for knowing how to juggle those myriad responsibilities and expectations that accompany a faculty position."[55] They write that mentoring can be one of the best experiences for teachers and students because it can cultivate and expand views of professional and personal success. Mentoring, for writing practitioners, is most generative when mentoring relationships are built on mutual benefit and respect. And yet, mentoring is far more complex than any other type of professional development initiative or relationship with a coach, counselor, guide, or tutor. Mentoring is not one-sided, it is reciprocal; it spans across positive, negative, and indifferent experiences, and it is informed by the personal, historical, and cultural identity categories that *both* mentor and mentee claim.

Mentoring in writing studies is commonly found in teacher training and graduate student support.[56] Mentoring is also understood in writing studies as an academic activity, that is, as the relationship between and/or among professors and students.[57] While this body of scholarship is useful to this chapter, the complexities associated with mentoring in non-traditional or alternative living/learning spaces, non-academic environments, and for career-long development have largely gone unaddressed. With few exceptions, much of the scholarship on mentoring in writing studies does not directly address if or how women and other marginalized groups mentor or are mentored beyond the classroom and other academic settings.[58]

Writing studies recognizes that mentoring is positioned as the relationship between or among persons who come together for the purpose of advising, guiding, or training one another. Mentoring often consists of two or more individuals who are interested in reciprocal interactions and activities that allow both personal and professional growth, while simultaneously acknowledging a balance of power that flows from the mentor to the mentee.[59] Mentoring can afford individuals opportunities to communicate with one another (both verbally and written), share thoughts, feelings, concerns, questions, and other information with one another, thereby potentially transforming professional and personal productivity for both the mentor and mentee. An investment approach to mentoring makes visible the often invisibility of power in mentoring relationships. And one way this framework begins to uncover power dynamics in mentoring is by prioritizing mentor and mentee gender identity in mentoring.

Academic scholarship in the social sciences and the humanities calls attention to a traditional model of mentoring, where masculinist values of competition directly influence (both negatively and positively) levels of professional activity and productivity.[60] In this way, an older, more-experienced expert helps a younger, less-experienced novice navigate various institutional situations. While this model of mentoring presents itself in rhetoric and writing, and in non-academic spaces too, alternative models of mentoring exist, which challenge traditional ways of mentoring and professionalization. For example, a commitment to feminist values of reciprocity, self-reflexivity (or self-awareness), and transparency can help mentors and mentees locate and use non-oppressive practices in mentoring relationships.

Women's studies theorist Christy Chandler writes that "research on mentors suggests that mentoring relationships provide a unique perspective on career development in a variety of fields and vocations," and yet much of that research is concerned with the male experience of mentoring, which does not necessarily reflect female or other minority groups' experiences of mentoring.[61] Chandler notes that there are typically two functions of traditional, hierarchical mentoring. Of the two functions, she writes,

> The first is a career-enhancing function that includes sponsorship (e.g., nominating a protégé for promotion), coaching (e.g., suggesting work strategies), facilitating exposure and visibility (e.g., bringing a protégé to meetings and conferences), offering challenging work, and protecting a protégé from criticism. All of these roles help the protégé establish credibility in the organization and prepare for advancement. The second is the psychosocial function, which involves the mentor as a role model, counselor, and friend and helps the young adult develop a sense of personal identity and competence.[62]

This master/apprentice approach to mentoring may benefit both the mentor and mentee in particular environments and situations, especially in terms of physical safety. Still, traditional mentoring practices often do not recognize the gender identities of mentor and mentee as valuable attributes to mentoring and its outcomes. In other words, as HTI and RCAH participants will demonstrate, failure to identify, recognize, and accept the influence of gender identity in the mentoring relationship suppresses desired learning outcomes and growth. By shifting writing practice to focus on *how* mentoring is invented, writing teachers and researchers can better recognize, address, and re-evaluate potential power imbalances that could be part of the relationship.

No doubt, imbalances of power are found within traditional mentoring models and individual mentoring relationships. Gail McGuire and Jo Reger advocate for a co-mentoring model, a model that is grounded in feminist theory and pedagogy. Co-mentoring, they write, "challenges masculinist values of hierarchy, competition, and objectivity by emphasizing the importance of cooperative, non-hierarchical relationships for learning and development."[63] Moreover, "feminist co-mentoring seeks to dispel the view of the disembodied intellectual by attending to academics' familial, personal, and emotional needs," all of which affect mentoring and its outcomes.[64]

Despite the potential benefits of traditional mentoring (e.g., safety for the mentee, and/or credibility for the mentor), this kind of mentoring has its disadvantages and potentially harmful consequences. Most significantly, traditional mentoring can reinforce power imbalances between individuals because one person in the relationship often has a monopoly on knowledge, skills, and resources. Acknowledging and embracing the personal, historical, cultural, and even emotional tendencies of mentoring can support growth and development for both the mentor and mentee and distribute those resources more evenly in the relationship. Therefore, a co-mentoring model, with its emphasis on mutual empowerment, can better balance personal and professional aspects of both the mentor's and mentee's lives. Later in this study, a kind of co-mentoring model—an investment model of mentoring—is discussed in greater detail, which works best for HTI employees and RCAH alumni.

As I have shown in this chapter, scholars in both women's studies and in writing studies comment on the two most common models of mentoring present in institutional spaces and places: a traditional model of mentoring and an alternative or co-mentoring model of mentoring. While both models of mentoring have their affordances and limitations, McGuire and Reger assert that their co-mentoring model can and should replace traditional mentoring relationships that often prevent women from working together.[65] All too common in work and/or other professional environments, women are "encouraged to build barriers between themselves instead of working cooperatively in predominately male departments."[66] Values of reciprocity, self-reflexivity (or self-awareness), and transparency can be part of how mentoring is invented in workplace cultures. Chapter 5 will address if and how those values build inclusivity instead of barriers between or among women and other marginalized groups of people.

Rhetoric and writing teachers and researchers often do and talk about mentoring in terms of formal and informal approaches to mentoring, and traditional and alternative models of mentoring. Mentoring, whether formal or informal, can manifest in many ways. While mentoring may begin as hierarchical, it can evolve toward a co-equal relationship because of work and community relationships, and even through socializing and friendship-building activities (like talking, listening, and going out for drinks after work). Further, even though mentoring relationships can be informal (i.e., not mandated by workplaces, departments, or programs), mentoring happens in ways both explicitly and implicitly, often at the same time (like asking a peer or superior for help on a task), and in a multitude of spaces and with many and varied tools and technologies. Ultimately, rhetoric and writing practitioners must continue to advocate for and create spaces within their departments that promote conversations about how writing in school settings prepares students for writing on the job. An investment approach to mentoring can facilitate these conversations and help student writers adjust to new and exciting school and workplace writing tasks and relationship-building situations.

So far, in this book, I have started to develop a heuristic for locating and inventing mentoring that is culturally and socially situated. What emerges from this heuristic is investment mentoring, a unique approach to mentoring that makes space for the self-identification of an individual who is part of a mentoring relationship. Chapters 4 and 5 will develop investment mentoring further by taking up Johndan Johnson-Eilola's call to writing studies for an increase in collaboration among socially and culturally aware learners, writers, and communicators.[67] He writes,

> By attempting to both learn from and change existing collaborative practices, we position ourselves and our students as socially responsible experts—in other words, we help students learn to be both effective participants and responsible community members.[68]

An investment approach to mentoring extends Johnson-Eilola's call and can also begin to shed light on Ginny Redish's charge by articulating what it means to "add value" as a technical and professional writer and communicator and how to do it.[69]

This framework can help participants at HTI and RCAH be both effective and responsible coworkers and community members. The experiences that participants share in the next five chapters illuminate the celebrations and challenges with using mentoring to learn about, build, and sustain productive and healthy workplace relationships. In turn, their stories and experiences of mentoring can help writing researchers and teachers theorize how mentoring impacts their everyday teaching and professionalization practices inside and out of the classroom.

Notes

1. Merriam-Webster's Dictionary Online, "Invention," accessed May 17, 2018, www. merriam-webster.com/dictionary/invention.
2. Merriam-Webster's Dictionary Online, "Investment."

3. Jacqueline Jones Royster and Gesa Kirsch, *Feminist Rhetorical Practices: New Horizons for Rhetoric, Composition, and Literacy Studies* (Carbondale: SIU Press, 2012).
4. Jones Royster and Kirsch, *Feminist*, 644.
5. Patti Lather, "Research as Praxis," *Harvard Educational Review* 56, no. 3 (September 1986); Gloria Anzaldúa, *Borderlands/La Frontera: The New Mestiza* (San Francisco: Aunt Lute Books, 1987); Linda Tuhiwai Smith, *Decolonizing Methodologies: Research and Indigenous Peoples* (London: Zed Books, 1999); Walter Mignolo, *The Darker Side of Western Modernity: Global Futures, Decolonial Options* (Durham: Duke University Press Books, 2011); and Malea Powell, "Dreaming Charles Eastman: Cultural Memory, Autobiography, and Geography in Indigenous Histories," in *Beyond the Archives: Research as a Lived Process*, eds. Gesa Kirsch and Liz Rohan (Carbondale: Southern Illinois University Press, 2008).
6. Janice Redish, "Adding Value as a Technical Communicator," *Technical Communication* 42, no. 1 (1995); Johndan Johnson-Eilola, "Relocating the Value of Work: Technical Communication in a Post-industrial Age," *Technical Communication Quarterly* 5, no. 3 (1996); James Henry, "Documenting Contributory Expertise: The Value Added By Technical Communicators in Collaborative Writing Situations," *Technical Communication* 45, no. 2 (1998); Jay Mead, "Measuring the Value Added By Technical Documentation: A Review of Research and Practice," *Technical Communication* 45, no. 3 (1998).
7. Bernadette Longo, "An Approach for Applying Cultural Study Theory to Technical Writing Research," *Technical Communication Quarterly* 7, no. 1 (1998): 11.
8. Longo, "An Approach," 12–14.
9. Angela Haas, "A Rhetoric of Alliance: What American Indians Can Tell Us About Digital and Visual Rhetoric" (Doctoral Dissertation, Michigan State University, 2008).
10. Stuart Hall, "Cultural Identity and Diaspora," *Framework*, no. 36 (1989): 222.
11. Hall, "Cultural," 225.
12. Hall, "Cultural," 225.
13. Haas, "A Rhetoric," 65.
14. Longo, "An Approach," 1.
15. Carolyn Miller, "A Humanistic Rationale for Technical Writing," *College English* 40, no. 6 (February 1979).
16. Miller, "A Humanistic," 610.
17. Sam Dragga and Dan Voss also discuss these points in "Cruel Pies: The Inhumanity of Technical Illustrations," *Technical Communication* 48, no. 3 (2001).
18. Miller, "A Humanistic," 617.
19. Carl G. Herndl, "Teaching Discourse and Reproducing Culture: A Critique of Research and Pedagogy in Professional and Non-academic Writing," *College Composition and Communication* 44 (1993): 350.
20. Herndl, "Teaching," 353.
21. Herndl, "Teaching," 354.
22. Herndl, "Teaching," 352.
23. Longo, "An Approach,"; Patricia Sullivan, "Visual Markers for Navigating Instructional Texts," *Journal of Technical Writing and Communication* 20, no. 3 (1990); Nancy Blyler, "Taking a Political Turn: The Critical Perspective and Research in Professional Communication," *Technical Communication Quarterly* 7 (1998).

24. Blake J. Scott and Bernadette Longo, "Guest Editors' Introduction: Making the Cultural Turn," *Technical Communication Quarterly* 15 (2006): 3.
25. Scott and Longo, "Guest Editors' Introduction," 8.
26. Michel Foucault, *The Archaeology of Knowledge* (Paris: Éditions Gallimard, 1972), 229.
27. Foucault, "The Archaeology," 230.
28. Longo, "An Approach," 8–11.
29. Michel de Certeau, *The Practice of Everyday Life* (Berkeley: University of California Press, 1984); Anzaldúa, *Borderlands*; Tuhiwai Smith, *Decolonizing*; Malea Powell, "Listening to Ghosts: An Alternative (non)Argument," in *ALT DIS: Alternative Discourses and the Academy*, eds. Christopher Schroeder, Helen Fox, and Patricia Bizzell (Portsmouth: Heinemann, 2002); Walter Mignolo, *The Darker Side of the Renaissance: Literacy, Territoriality, & Colonization* (Ann Arbor: University of Michigan Press, 2003); Mignolo, *The Darker Side of Western*; and Angela Haas, "Race, Rhetoric, and Technology: A Case Study of Decolonial Technical Communication Theory, Methodology and Pedagogy," *Journal of Business and Technical Communication* 26, no. 3 (2012).
30. de Certeau, *The Practice*; Tuhiwai Smith, *Decolonizing*; Haas, "Race."
31. de Certeau, *The Practice*.
32. de Certeau, *The Practice*, xi.
33. de Certeau, *The Practice*, xi, 30.
34. de Certeau, *The Practice*, 37.
35. de Certeau, *The Practice*, 36.
36. Jean-Francois Lyotard, *The Postmodern Condition: A Report on Knowledge* (Minneapolis: University Of Minnesota Press, 1984).
37. Tuhiwai Smith, *Decolonizing*.
38. Tuhiwai Smith, *Decolonizing*, 4.
39. Tuhiwai Smith, *Decolonizing*, 4.
40. Tuhiwai Smith, *Decolonizing*, 20.
41. Haas, "Race."
42. Haas, "Race," 279.
43. Haas, "Race," 288.
44. Haas, "Race," 280; Steven Katz, "The Ethic of Expediency: Classical Rhetoric, Technology, and the Holocaust," *College English* 54 (1992); Jennifer Slack, David Miller, and Jeffrey Doak, "The Technical Communicator as Author: Meaning, Power, Authority," *Journal of Business and Technical Communication* 7 (1993).
45. Haas, "Race," 284.
46. Haas," Race," 297.
47. Merriam-Webster Dictionary Online, "Mentor," accessed May 18, 2018, www.merriam-webster.com/dictionary/mentor.
48. Michelle F. Eble and Lynée Lewis Gaillet, *Stories of Mentoring: Theory and Praxis* (West Lafayette: Parlor Press, 2008): 311.
49. Eble and Lewis Gaillet, *Stories*, 7.
50. Jennifer Clary-Lemon and Duane Roen, "Webs of Mentoring in Graduate School," in *Stories of Mentoring: Theory & Praxis*, eds. Lynee Lewis Gaillet and Michelle F. Eble (West Lafayette: Parlor Press, 2008); Lynn Bloom, "Mentoring as Mosaic: Life as Guerilla Theater," *Composition Studies* 35, no. 2 (2007).
51. Clary-Lemon and Roen, "Webs," 178.
52. Cindy Moore, "A Letter to Graduate Student Women on Mentoring," *Profession* (2000): 149.

53. Moore, "A Letter," 152–154.
54. Wendy Sharer, Jessica Enoch, and Cheryl Glenn, "Performing Professionalism: On Mentoring and Being Mentored," in *Stories of Mentoring: Theory & Praxis*, eds. Lynee Lewis Gaillet and Michelle F. Eble. (West Lafayette: Parlor Press, 2008).
55. Sharer, Enoch, and Glenn, "Performing," 129.
56. Sally Barr Ebest, "Mentoring: Past, Present, and Future," in *Preparing College Teachers of Writing: Histories, Theories, Programs, and Practices*, eds. Betty Pytlik and Sarah Liggett (New York: Oxford University Press, 2002); Samantha Blackmon and Shirley Rose, "Plug and Play: Technology and Mentoring of Teaching Assistants," in *Don't Call It That: The Composition Practicum*, ed. Sid Dobrin (Urbana: NCTE, 2005).
57. Scott Miller, Brenda Jo Bruegemann, Bennis Blue, and Deneen M. Shepherd, "Present Perfect," *College Composition and Communication* 48, no. 3 (1997); Bloom, "Mentoring as Mosaic"; Clary-Lemon and Roen, "Webs of Mentoring"; Ken Baake, Stephen A. Bernhardt, Eve R. Brumberger, Katherine Durack, Bruce Farmer, Julie Dyke Ford, Thomas Hager, Robert Kramer, Lorelei Ortiz, and Carolyn Vickery, "Mentorship, Collegiality, and Friendship: Making Our Mark as Professionals," in *Stories of Mentoring: Theory & Praxis*, eds. Lynee Lewis Gaillet and Michelle F. Eble (West Lafayette: Parlor Press, 2008).
58. Christy Chandler, "Mentoring Women in Academia: Reevaluating the Traditional Model," *NWSA Journal* 8, no. 3 (1996); Moore, "A Letter"; Rebecca Rickly and Susanmarie Harrington, "Feminist Approaches to Mentoring Teaching Assistants: Conflict, Power, and Collaboration," in *Preparing College Teachers of Writing: Histories, Theories, Programs, and Practices*, eds. Betty Pytlik and Sarah Liggett (New York: Oxford University Press, 2002); Gail McGuire and Jo Reger, "Feminist Co-Mentoring: A Model for Academic Professional Development," *NWSA Journal* 15, no. 1 (2003); Lisa Ede, *Situating Composition: Composition Studies and the Politics of Location* (Carbondale: SIU Press, 2004); Sharer, Enoch, and Glenn, "Performing"; and Pamela VanHaitsma and Steph Ceraso, "'Making It' in the Academy Through Horizontal Mentoring," *Peitho* 19, no. 2 (2017).
59. Bloom, "Mentoring as Mosaic"; Baake et al., "Mentorship, Collegiality"; Barbara Cole and Arabella Lyon, "Mentor or Magician: Reciprocities, Existing Ideologies, and Reflections of a Discipline," in *Stories of Mentoring: Theory & Praxis*, eds. Lynee Lewis Gaillet and Michelle F. Eble (West Lafayette: Parlor Press, 2008); Cinda Coggins Mosher and Mary Trachsel, "Panopticism? Or Just Paying Attention?" in *Stories of Mentoring: Theory & Praxis*, eds. Lynee Lewis Gaillet and Michelle F. Eble (West Lafayette: Parlor Press, 2008).
60. Geraldine McNenny and Duane Roen, "The Case for Collaborative Scholarship in Rhetoric and Composition," *Rhetoric Review* (1992); Mary Ann Cain, "Mentoring as Identity Exchange: Conflicts and Connections," *Feminist Teacher* 8, no. 3 (1994); Gail Y. Okawa, "Diving for Pearls: Mentoring as Cultural and Activist Practice Among Academics of Color," *College Composition and Communication* 53, no. 3 (February 2002); Bloom, "Mentoring as Mosaic"; James Henry and Holly Huff Bruland, "Educating Reflexive Practitioners: Casting Graduate Teaching Assistants as Mentors in First-Year Classrooms," *International Journal of Teaching and Learning in Higher Education* 22, no. 3 (2010); Robert Stowers and Robert Barker, "The Coaching and Mentoring Process: The

Obvious Knowledge and Skill Set for Organizational Communication Professors," *Journal of Technical Writing and Communication* 40 (2010).
61. Chandler, "Mentoring," 79.
62. Chandler, "Mentoring," 81.
63. McGuire and Reger, "Feminist," 54.
64. McGuire and Reger, "Feminist," 54.
65. McGuire and Reger, "Feminist."
66. McGuire and Reger, "Feminist," 62.
67. Johnson-Eilola, "Relocating."
68. Johnson-Eilola, "Relocating," 260.
69. Redish, "Adding," 505.

3 A Feminist Methodological Approach for Locating and Inventing Mentoring

> Stories, like good theories, make connections that may not at first glance seem straightforward.
> —Julie Cruikshank, *The Social Life of Stories: Narrative and Knowledge in the Yukon Territory*

This chapter proposes an approach to locate, uncover, and be responsible to the questions raised in Chapter 2. Specifically, I illustrate how to enact a feminist methodological approach for discovering and creating investment mentoring. This framework holds me accountable to the practices I claimed for such research, and the communities in and for which my work was done. Writing studies practitioners will gain valuable insight into conducting research on workplace and classroom mentoring, or other such studies that are similarly focused on community outreach and professional development.

In recent years, rhetoric and writing studies scholars have become more interested in writing as it intersects with professional development and mentoring. In the last twenty years, published analyses on writing and professional development have been more common; there has been close study of the disconnect between academic and workplace writing; a critical examination on how power, knowledge, and texts are generated and reproduced over time in a workplace; and a study on why genre and writing technologies matter in a workplace.[1] Equally important is the scholarship on professional development, mentoring, and workplace relationship building, particularly the research that addresses academic work experiences and academic mentoring.[2] While this body of writing studies research concerning power, writing, and workplace relationship building informs this study, the studies mentioned above do not explicitly address how individuals use mentoring to learn over the duration of their career. To help remedy this gap in writing studies scholarship, this study closely examined how mentoring helps individuals stay accountable to and responsible for the kinds of writing, communication, and relationship-building practices in their workplaces. This chapter focuses on how those relationship-building practices are found and developed, and how they affect a person's ability to construct, maintain, and express their identity.

Rhetoric is the study of networks of meaning-making, and these meaning-making practices include writing, composing, and performing. This way of understanding rhetoric positions mentoring as a critical component of an individual's ability to learn, process, and retain information. Mentoring also aids in helping a person convert the information they have learned into useable and transferrable knowledge over the duration of their career. In short, mentoring is a set of strategic rhetorical practices or rhetorical work, the kind of work that aids in an individual's career-long, experiential learning. Mentoring is rhetorical work that can be located through observations, interviews, and mapping or diagramming a person's professional and personal networks.

This chapter details the plan used for studying mentoring at HealthTech Industries (HTI or HealthTech) and the Residential College in the Arts in Humanities (RCAH) at Michigan State University (MSU). This frame is enacted to show how workplace learning and relationships are sustained at HTI and in RCAH. The methodologies and methods in this chapter connect workplace learning and workplace relationship building to the mentoring a person experiences throughout their career. Further, this approach to locating, examining, and inventing mentoring in the workplace is illustrated as a powerful means to success over the many years an individual develops professionally and personally. What is articulated is a set of practices that reveal how mentoring is rhetorical, that is how mentoring is composed of a set of relational practices that can be used for building and maintaining moments of experiential learning.

HTI and the RCAH

HTI is a medical device and case and tray manufacturing company with locations all over the world. The research site for this book is one of HTI's main campuses located in the Midwest, USA. HTI is part of a small yet vibrant community that is politically, religiously, and socially conservative. For many of the HTI participants, the surrounding community and physical location were crucial in their decision to work for HealthTech.

> One of the things I wanted to do with my family is to be able to have a place that we could call home. That became important to me the longer I was married. We came back to [the area] because we felt like it was a

good place to be able to call home, a great place to be able to raise kids. It had the economic support here with the medical and manufacturing industries that created a good living for people in the community.

There really is a lot to do here. We have theater, we have concerts, and then we are just a couple of hours away from bigger cities. We have all that the bigger cities have to offer, museums and culture and all that. I think this area is a great place to raise children. I don't have children, but I know that the school system and what it has to offer is phenomenal. We even have lakes!

HealthTech's main campus is composed of two manufacturing buildings. The first building, known as building one by employees, houses executive and management offices in the front one-third of the building and manufacturing spaces in the remaining two-thirds. The employees in building one produce human resources policies, other documents related to managing large-scale projects, materials related to medical implants and instruments, and the implants and instruments themselves. The second building, building two, produces cases and trays for the implants and instruments made in building one. In building two, there are a few smaller offices for management-level employees, but the majority of the space is for machinery and production equipment. Each building has a lobby with receptionist area, and a number of different sized conference rooms for meetings. Despite the buildings' similarities, it is obvious that much of the business conducted at HTI happens in building one. There are marked differences in each building (e.g., number of executive offices, the kinds of administrative technologies); however, these differences are not the subject of this study, although they may contribute to participants' experiences of mentoring at work.

HTI participants work in different company divisions at HealthTech and have worked at HealthTech for at least ten years, with some participants working at HealthTech for twenty or more years. To maintain participants' anonymity, any references to the kinds of work participants do at HealthTech is noted as executive, management, senior-level, or some combination of these terms. Participants for this study were recruited in two phases over the course of two academic years, and then they were separated into two groups: the first and primary group was HTI employees, and the second group was RCAH alumni. HTI participants for this study were initially recruited through Julie, an employee at HealthTech, and a professional contact of mine prior to this study. I emailed Julie and asked her if we could have a phone conversation so that I could explain the general design and purpose of the study. After my initial conversation with Julie, she emailed a list of employee names and email addresses to me. The employees on the list were curious about the study, and ulti-mately interested in participating in it. After I sent individual emails to each HTI employee on the list, seven additional HTI employees agreed to participate in this study, for a total of eight HTI participants, four women and four men. Interestingly, each HTI participant recruited for this study occupied some kind of executive, managerial, or administrative position at HealthTech. Later in this chapter, I discuss the methods I used when working with HTI participants.

What is more, the RCAH focuses exclusively on issues that matter most to arts and humanities students and faculty. The residential college is built on four central themes: world history, arts and culture, ethics, and civic engagement. Students live and learn in a custom-built environment that includes their own dorm rooms, cafeteria, classrooms, theater, art studio, gallery, language and media center, and music practice rooms. Their class sizes are typically small (with no more than twelve to fifteen students in a class), which can provide students with an intimate space for more in-depth conversations about current events that interest them. I cover the methods I used with RCAH alumni in Chapter 6.

On Storytelling, Rhetorical Listening, and Mapping

The methods used in this study reflect my commitment to qualitative and cultural research practices. The framework for this study adheres to three broader concepts for carrying out such research:

1. storytelling,
2. rhetorical listening, and
3. mapping.

This framework helps rhetoric and writing practitioners to not only value what mentoring is and why it is important in workplaces (e.g., job satisfac-tion and career enhancement, or possible advancement and job promotion), but to also value how these practices—these relationships—are located, invented, and understood in the first place. As I stated in Chapter 1, this book is a rhetorical analysis of workplace mentoring and workplace rela-tionship building. And rhetoric and writing researchers and teachers can learn from this example that the invention of workplace relationships and mentoring networks depends on the stories and histories employees share with one another, that they tell themselves, and that they ask their friends and families to believe.

My decision to foreground participant voices in this study is similar to other workplace writing and relationship building scholarship in writing studies and technical communication studies.[3] Patricia Sullivan and James Porter write that researchers must be reflective of the methodological choices they make in their research.[4] The methods and rationale for using such methods must be purposeful, thoughtful, and appropriate to the context of research and work with and for the communities involved. Researchers must "embrace working across methodological interfaces . . . to expand critically and creatively the boundaries of research."[5] Doing anything less greatly damages the larger goal of all research, which is "to help empower and liberate through the act and art of writing."[6]

To these ends, I made an important decision designing this study—to prioritize participants' stories of mentoring in a way that highlighted their daily, lived experiences of mentoring instead of *only* reporting on the written or otherwise recorded mentoring practices, procedures, or policies. The function of participant voice throughout this study—the first broader research concept noted previously—showcases the efforts of everyone involved, from participants to myself. My decision to conduct research in this way calls attention to the "effort [that] stresses their [participants'] bodies, and ours," which can be accomplished by using a feminist' research methodology.[7]

Discussing workplace stories, relationships, and mentoring can be potentially harmful to participants' personal well-being and job security. However, acknowledging their positions through individual voice is not only necessary, but also acts as a way to be accountable to participants' and my commitments to doing research well. Each chapter in this book is framed because of and around participants' experiences with mentoring. In doing so, I laid out a plan for doing research about mentoring that provides a diverse view of how mentoring is invented and sustained in workplace cultures.

Feminist research practices, according to social and political theorists Liz Stanley and Sue Wise, must be concerned with all aspects of social reality and all participants in it.[8] The social reality for HTI and RCAH participants is that the personal is political. And this belief (that the personal is also political), is one that is central to all waves and kinds of feminism. It underscores nearly every story found in this book. And further still, Stanley and Wise note,

> The personal is not only the political. It is also the crucial variable which is absolutely present in each and every attempt to "do research," although it is frequently invisible in terms of the presentation of this research. It mustn't be absent from presentations of feminist research, because this is to deny the importance of the personal elsewhere. In other words, academic feminism must take feminist beliefs seriously,

by integrating these within our research. We see the presence of the researcher's self as central in all research.[9]

Participant and researcher personhood cannot be left behind or intentionally excluded in research; personhood cannot be left out of the research process and full use of it must be made. Therefore, the framework for this book included—indeed it insisted upon—me sharing my experiences with mentoring in professional places with participants. HealthTech and RCAH participants' experiences of mentoring come from and are built around their past and current mentoring or other professional development experiences. A participant's past and current experiences with mentoring, for instance, create new understandings of what mentoring is and how it is legitimized in their workplace culture. What is learned, then, is how different accounts of mentoring accumulate over time, and how those accumulations inform, reflect, and reinforce the beliefs, values, politics, and histories of that workplace.[10] Ultimately, the work of a person investing in their professional identity aids in sustainable organizational relationships.

The traditions, expectations, or lore of a workplace can cause a person to consent to or challenge the hierarchies in which they work. A person can also work to confirm or eliminate biases of gender identity, race, class, and ability in their personal and professional spaces.[11] The narrative mentoring experiences of HTI and RCAH participants are the foundation of this study's methodology; their stories articulate and affirm how mentoring is located, understood, and invented in their workplace, and also the affordances and consequences of those practices for individual and company success.

Participants' stories of mentoring illustrate, as Thomas King notes, how stories have shaped their ways of being and doing at home, at work, and in society.[12] Their stories shape their personal beliefs and impact their individual and collective workplace decisions. The stories participants tell and choose to believe about mentoring form not only their attitudes toward professional development and mentoring, but also their current and future mentoring relationships and practices. Their stories challenge previous understandings of mentoring as an object of study and instead move toward an understanding of mentoring as a culturally significant set of practices that are always already relational and professional.

As HTI and RCAH participants shared their stories of mentoring with me, they were audio recorded, and then those recordings were listened to and transcribed. Krista Ratcliffe's *Rhetorical Listening: Identification, Gender, Whiteness* was especially useful in helping me closely examine my personal, cultural, and professional values as they related to participants' stories of mentoring.[13] Rhetorical listening—the second broader research concept noted earlier in this chapter—is one way to negotiate "always-evolving standpoints and identities, with the always-evolving standpoints of others."[14] The stories in this book are permeable positions that "are not autonomous points of static stasis but rather complex webs of dynamically intermingled cultural structures and subjective agency."[15] By using rhetorical listening, I constructed and modeled a practice that is impartial and dynamic, a practice that HTI employees and RCAH alumni can use to foster deliberate self-identifications that may facilitate the sustainability of their professional relationships.

The third and final component for locating mentoring in a workplace is mapping. The mapping HTI participants did consisted of them drawing a map of their mentoring network—that is, on a sheet of paper, each participant drew a diagram or network tree of the people, places, and things that they associate with mentoring.[16] The affordances of a mentoring map or network are twofold. First, this mapping exercise gave participants a way to visually, alphabetically, and non-alphabetically represent their experiences of and attitudes toward mentoring. Visual representations, as Clay Spinuzzi writes, show how things, places, ideas, and people "from different functional areas collaborate to solve problems, connecting in networks, that include different tools, objectives, rules, and divisions of labor, tools, and artifacts."[17] Second, when used *with* storytelling and rhetorical listening, mapping can help writing practitioners understand how an individual's relationship to and with ideas, artifacts, and other people encourage or limit different kinds of professional knowledge and practices in their work environment. By using maps for collecting experiences of mentoring, participants made more visible the textual and literal geographies of their work environment, and the mentoring experiences and work histories that most matter to them. Mapping or diagramming helps HTI employees make more obvious the cultures claimed as home, personal, and professional, and if, how, where, and why those cultures intersect.

Participants' mentoring maps are contextual and deliberate articulations of their past and present mentoring experiences. Each map shows the people, places, ideas, emotions, and things that influence their mentoring. As each participant drew their mentoring map, they told stories of personal and professional development. They connected their verbal mentoring stories to other personal and professional relationships (e.g., spousal interactions and interactions with coworkers), professional expectations (e.g., promotion within the company), and cultural artifacts (e.g., an email indicating a social mentoring get-together). Maps can help individuals and writing studies teachers and researchers position mentoring as always-already active by focusing on its mobile nature, and not only its ability to be seen, talked about, or listened to. Mapping afforded participants to visually represent how mentoring is, as Spinuzzi suggests "circulated, transformed, displaced, hybridized, and developed to meet the needs of particular, localized work."[18]

In the second chapter of this book, I situated teaching and mentoring in writing studies in the larger conversations about what it means to invest in and invent mentoring. In the beginning of this chapter, I detailed the qualitative frame I designed to see mentoring and professional development in rhetoric and writing practice differently. The remainder of this chapter is used to elaborate on the set of methods I used to carry out the research for this study. These methods are aligned with the theory and methodologies that inform this study; they correspond to the framework discussed in this chapter. So, to better understand how mentoring is invented in a workplace, I adhered to four different methods of story and information collection, and each focused on participants' experiences of mentoring:

1. field observations,
2. individual interviews,
3. participant-drawn mentoring maps, and
4. focus group interviews.

I toured building one (implants and instruments) first and then building two (trays and cases) at HealthTech's main campus. During my observations of both buildings, I was able to get a feel for the kinds of activities in and across the buildings. These observations also helped me contextualize the kinds of work participants would later talk about in their individual and focus group interviews. All eight HTI participants agreed to be interviewed for the study; however, because of the competitive nature of HealthTech's work, all eight employees declined to be observed in their offices during one 8–10 hour workday. Despite this hiccup, I asked HTI participants to fill out a worksheet with questions pertaining to their daily and weekly work and communication activities. Several of the HTI employees completed the worksheet, and their responses inform later chapters in this study. While I do not know why some of the HTI employees did not complete their workplace communication worksheet, I assumed that those employees simply forgot to complete the requested task. Still, while I was not able to observe HTI participants for one workday, they did agree to be interviewed about the kinds of work they do during a typical workday.

Participants' individual interviews were coded at three different levels: the idea level, the paragraph level, and the sentence level. These coded items made visible interesting and unique workplace relationship patterns, which later formed the fourth method for this study, focus groups. The third method in this study, participant-drawn mentoring maps, occurred during the individual interviews. During the individual interviews, I asked participants to draw their mentoring maps, and indicate the people, things, beliefs and values, and places that factor into their mentoring and other professional development practices. Lastly, four months after the last individual interview was completed, I conducted two focus groups with HTI participants, which addressed the patterns that arose during their individual interviews. I conducted two focus groups with six HTI participants in total. The three HTI participants who did not participate in the focus groups were either out of town or had conflicting schedules that coincided with the timing of the groups.

What follows is a detailed analysis of my time spent with HealthTech participants about their experiences with professional development and mentoring. My analysis attempts to answer Eble and Lewis Gaillet's challenge to writing studies practitioners to not only acknowledge and celebrate differences in mentoring—differences that occur across boundaries of race, class, gender, and ability—but also to cultivate and promote mutual benefit and respect between and among all involved in mentoring.[19] Additionally, I briefly articulate the challenges of researching an investment approach to mentoring.

The methods I used in this study are a means to explore mentoring as situated, as contextually bound in time, space, and in participants' stories of mentoring and work. Even with their stories, as with all research, there may appear to be gaps in this study. For example, the eight HTI participants are a small representation of HealthTech, and do not necessarily represent other employees who work there. Further, about half way through interviewing HTI participants, several other HTI employees voiced their interest in participating in the study. And while such additions would have been enjoyable and a way to gain a more accurate representation of mentoring at HealthTech, I could not add to this study due to the limited time, resources, and scope of the study. The stories and experiences of the participants in this study provided a small but nevertheless important snapshot into the professionalization practices and mentoring relationships for HealthTech employees.

The owner of HealthTech was interested in and supportive of the research being done with and for his company. He was not interviewed for the study, but was provided with a general research findings report or executive summary after the data collection and analysis period was completed. In the findings report, I highlighted how employees understand and invent mentoring at HealthTech. Then, during a conversation in August 2014 between him and me, we discussed how mentoring matters to the employees at HealthTech. During our time together, we brainstormed strategies specific to HTI for sustaining and improving employees' professional development experiences at work. I was encouraged to have the support of the owner for this study; however, it was clear to me going into this study that a fine line exists between a boss endorsing research and a boss requiring employees to participate. Nevertheless, it was exciting to have the owner's sincere support for this study. He found genuine favor with my study because it made actionable company values associated with mentoring, career-long learning, and sustainable workplace relationships.

Moreover, this study did not seek to characterize every type of mentoring relationship or experience at HealthTech, but it focused instead on what rhetoric and writing can learn about investment mentoring for sustainable, career-long learning. HTI and RCAH participants in this study were recruited because they had expressed, at one time or another in their careers, interest and participation in professional development and mentoring initiatives and programs.

In Chapter 2, I suggested that writing studies might understand mentoring as cultural, relational, and rhetorical—as a set of meaning-making tactics that keep individuals accountable and responsible to their writing, communication, and learning practices. With these ideas in mind, it may have been prudent of me to note other moments, texts, or documents that factored into mentoring for employees at HealthTech (e.g., monthly/quarterly division meetings, HR documents). However, by focusing solely on HTI and RCAH participants' experiences of mentoring, I created a study with a controllable boundary that began to address what Eble and Lewis Gaillet have called for researchers and teachers to do.[20] My study:

1. focused expressly on those HTI and RCAH participants' mentoring relationships more broadly, and
2. detailed the relational aspects of participants' networks.

The narrow focus on HTI and RCAH participants' mentoring relationships directed this study by taking a closer look at the tensions, problems, celebrations, and challenges that can arise from employee self-identification, career-long learning, and workplace relationships. This study did not directly take up how employees use mentoring to navigate other workplace networks (e.g., technology networks, financial networks, supply chain networks), how digital and online technologies affect mentoring, or the effects of space and place on mentoring relationships and practices.[21] These themes should certainly be explored in future writing studies research.

Fieldnotes and General Observations

Prior to working with HealthTech employees, I knew very little about the company. It was not clear to me what employees did there, or what kinds of medical devices they produced and for whom. In fall of 2013, I established my connection with HealthTech, and the general structure of the study was briefly explained to Julie (who would later agree to be a participant in the study). I discussed the learning goals and outcomes of the study with Julie, as well as how the study satisfied the degree completion requirements for me; however, under no circumstances were HTI or RCAH employees required to participate in the study. Still, it was because of this initial phone conversation with Julie that other HTI employees were recruited for this project.

My first time at HTI was in February 2014, for field observations and the first three individual interviews. After arriving at building one, I introduced myself to the central administrative assistant, signed in, received a name badge and lanyard, and sat in the lobby for a few minutes. As I sat there waiting for Julie, I observed employees walking to and from one another's offices, customers and business partners coming and going to and from HealthTech, and also the names of people, meetings and their locations, and other technical jargon circulating throughout the building's intercom system. Shortly after I arrived at HealthTech, while I waited in the lobby, I asked to use a public restroom. After receiving directions to the restroom from the administrative assistant, I walked the halls of building one toward the restroom. As I walked, I observed the general layout of HTI offices, conference rooms, and the kitchen/dining space; I briefly experienced the atmosphere and tone of their work environment. Since I could not observe HTI participants for one workday, I recorded what I remembered from my quick observations of their company culture as I walked to and from the restroom. I recorded these notes on my laptop later that day after the interviews were completed. I applied this same strategy to the participant-led tours of buildings one and two.[22]

During the month of February 2014, I visited HealthTech for four, full days, over a two-week period to record participants' individual interviews. Then, in June and July 2014, I conducted focus groups with participants, and spent an additional six hours with them at HealthTech. The time I spent with HTI participants varied to accommodate their schedules, and also to make room for long interviews and focus group sessions. Among individual interviews, focus-group interviews, and social meetings with HTI participants and other HealthTech employees (e.g., lunches and coffee breaks with participants and other employees), I spent approximately thirty-five hours with HealthTech employees.

Methods with Individual Participants

To understand HTI participants' experiences and stories of mentoring, eight HealthTech employees were interviewed for the study, each of whom hold different kinds of executive and management-level positions within the company. The HTI participants in the study were: Maria, Claire, Julie, Kris, Bill, Patrick, Kevin, and Randall. In Chapters 4 and 5, participants tell contextualized stories about their experiences with mentoring, especially how they use mentoring to learn and write well, and also how mentoring helps them form and be accountable to their workplace relationships. But for now, in this chapter, the focus is on how I interacted with HTI employees so that the intricacies of how their mentoring practices are connected to their development as a professional are made clear. Rhetoric and writing practitioners can glean from this chapter one way to conduct research on mentoring.

Even though Julie was contacted prior to this study officially starting, I did not know who would be interviewed about their experiences with mentoring. What I did know was that the company invested in their employees' professional development and career growth; according to HealthTech's website, the company is committed to building *quality relationships first* and quality products second. HealthTech's commitment to relationships, which is the cornerstone of the company's vision and mission statements, came up during several individual interviews. I wanted to talk to anyone who wanted to share their mentoring stories, whether those stories were negative or positive. Ultimately, what I learned from working with HTI was their commitment to relationships is to *both* employees and customers.

My first interaction with HTI participants included the preparation for and completion of individual interviews with each person. A week prior to the scheduled interview times, I emailed the interview questions to participants, so that they could prepare for their interview. I wrote the interview questions to reflect my commitment to a feminist, qualitative methodology. This approach to interviewing asks the person being interviewed to reflect on a wide range of life experiences that may influence their present-day professional development practices and experiences. When I arrived at HealthTech to interview participants and tour the manufacturing buildings, I introduced myself and repeated a brief summary of the study, which was explained to them in the emails that were sent out previously asking for their participation in the study. I met with each participant alone, in either their office or private company conference room. Each interview lasted at least one hour, with some interviews lasting two or two-and-a-half hours. Our conversations were recorded using both a digital recording device and also a sound recording application on my personal computer. When appropriate, for example, if a participant said something important or worth remembering, I noted it in a Microsoft Word document and saved it on my computer.

While interviewing participants in a semi-structured, story-based way was an important part of the feminist, qualitative methodology used in this study, a limitation of this method was that some of the information I collected was possibly too far off topic (e.g., conversations about children, or about extracurricular activities) than was required for this study.[23] I found it somewhat difficult to sift through each transcribed interview to organize, code, and decide what to keep in and what to exclude from the written description of this study. Even though it took extra time in coding and analyzing participants' stories because of the nearly twenty-five hours of recorded stories, participants indicated that the interviews felt more like a conversation than an interview, that they enjoyed our time together, and that they were comfortable in sharing their experiences of mentoring and other sensitive workplace stories. For this reason alone—having participants feel comfortable during the interview sessions—I would replicate the interview strategies I used for any future research study.

Much of this study focused on how gender identity influences or shapes an individual's approach to mentoring. It was my top priority that participants could decide for themselves when to share things about their gender identity that affected their mentoring relationships and practices. For instance, if I asked a question that made a participant feel uncomfortable, I assured them that they did not have to answer the question and that their non-response would not affect the rest of their interview or the analysis of it. I frequently verbalized my interests in mentoring and identity development with HTI participants, so they were encouraged to share whatever stories they cared to share during our time together. Chapters 4 and 5 affirm that most HTI employees were comfortable talking about the gender identity and the ways it impacted their workplace relationships. Chapter 6 takes a closer look at mentoring for RCAH participants.

Despite my cautious yet open approach to interviewing participants, I found that five HTI participants (Maria, Claire, Randall, Julie, and Patrick) were comfortable talking about and/or relating their gender identity to their experiences with mentoring, professional development, and their general approaches to work at HealthTech. And all eight participants linked their experiences with and approach to mentoring to school learning and other non-school education. By the end of the eighth interview, it was clear to me that employees at HealthTech used mentoring as a way to not only continue their informal and formal education, but also to learn more about themselves and their commitments to building solid workplace and personal relationships.

I concluded each individual interview with two written activities, one to be completed at the end of the interview, and the other to be completed and snail-mailed or emailed back to me. In the first activity, I asked participants to draw their mentoring network maps. I explained to each participant what a mentoring map was, and I showed each person an example map. I also gave them verbal directions of what I wanted them to do. I supplied participants with an 8.5 inch x 11 inch sheet of white paper, and a pen and pencil for this activity. For the second activity, I gave each HTI participant a two-page worksheet to complete, which addressed their day-to-day work practices and workplace communication routines. The goal of this second activity was to get a better understanding of how each participant worked in their particular division, and how work, writing, communication, and mentoring intersect for them daily.

During individual interviews, I asked participants to draw their own mentoring network maps. I told participants to put their names in the middle of the sheet of paper, circle them, and then begin to build their maps with the people, ideas, places, and things they find useful for mentoring and professional development. Once they completed their map, I encouraged participants to rank what they drew on their map in order of importance (one being the most important). Participants were able to visualize and build their professional development network, and then use their maps to contextualize their individual and focus group interviews. Ultimately, the ranking or self-categorization of the people, ideas, places, and things HTI participants find most useful for successful mentoring makes visible for participants and others at HTI what is most valued personally and how those values match what is valued in the larger HealthTech community. Figure 3.1 is an example of a mentoring network map from one of the participants at HealthTech.

I received six out of eight participant mentoring network maps. Some participants completed their mentoring maps during their interviews, and others needed more time to complete their drawings, and so they snail-mailed or emailed their maps to me within a week of their interview. I did not receive two mentoring maps, and I assume this is simply because two participants forgot to complete the activity.

The second written activity I asked participants to complete was about their day-to-day work practices, and how they communicated with their colleagues. I came up with this activity because I knew ahead of time that I could not observe participants in their work environment for one workday because of privacy restrictions. As with the mentoring map activity, participants were under no obligation to complete this written activity. I received six out of eight participant workplace communication worksheets. Again, I believe I did not receive two communication activities because participants forgot to complete the task.

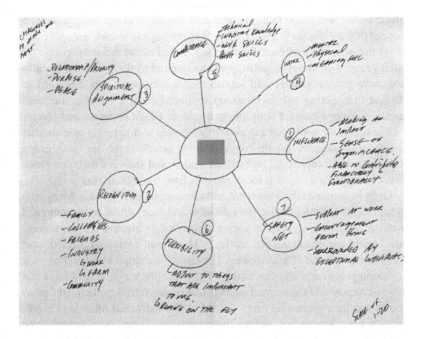

Figure 3.1

Photograph: Participant-Drawn Mentoring Map

Once I completed the individual interviews with participants, I transcribed, coded, sorted, and analyzed the interviews as well as their mentoring network maps and workplace communication worksheets. I determined that the workplace communication worksheets would not be used in this study because the focus of the study was on specific and significant stories about mentoring. Many participants' workplace communication worksheet responses did not articulate mentoring as such, but rather the intricacies of a participant's daily work routine, which can most certainly influence their mentoring practices and habits. Still, as a result of the coding and analysis of these three activities, I decided to conduct focus group interviews with participants. I placed participants into a focus group that was connected to a similar story of mentoring from another participant.

The second encounter I had with participants was during focus group sessions. The focus groups for this study occurred in June and July of 2014. As with the individual interviews, I emailed participants the focus group interview questions a week before, and I explained that the group would last no more than an hour. Interestingly enough, participants planned ahead and reserved at least two hours for the focus group sessions, and each focus group lasted two hours. In all, I conducted two focus group interviews with six out of the eight participants, three HTI employees in each group.

At the beginning of each focus group, I read aloud the instructions for each group. I encouraged participants to respond to the questions by talking more to one another and less to me. Surprisingly, they managed to do just that; during one focus group session, I observed that participants rarely made eye contact with me, and instead talked and gestured toward one another, all while writing down key points and drawing one another diagrams or pictures to help convey talking points. Once the focus group sessions were completed, I transcribed, coded, and analyzed their conversations. Some data from each focus group is used throughout this book.

Once I completed the individual and focus group interviews, I wrote analytical memos that addressed the interview and focus group conversations.[24] Analytical memos, sometimes known as qualitative memos, are short, mini-analyses of collected data and stories.[25] These mini-analyses reflected what I learned as a result of interviewing HealthTech employees and coding their mentoring network maps. Each memo was about one single-spaced page, and it was composed of themes and patterns that emerged from participants' interviews and their mentoring maps. Based on the individual interviews alone, in total, I wrote more than twenty-five analytical memos. Then, I categorized the analytical memos by locating moments where a participant's experience aligned with or challenged the research questions that framed this study.

After I wrote the analytical memos, I coded and sorted them according to participants' stories and other written data by using a listing exercise. The listing exercise was made up of three steps. First, I created a three-column spreadsheet in Microsoft Excel. In the first column, I wrote a list of the claims I could support with original data. These claims were straightforward and descriptive, and some were also obvious (e.g., mentoring happens at HealthTech). Every claim I made was supported by evidence from the interviews and written activities. This evidence made up the second column. In this second column, I referenced the analytical memo and also any secondary scholarship that would support or refute the claim. In column three, I referenced all of the primary source data collected that supported the claim. The primary data used to support these claims were found in transcribed interviews, fieldnotes, observations, written activities, and collected artifacts. I used one or more of these primary data throughout this study as evidence to support a claim; for example, a participant's mentoring network map served as evidence for *both* Chapters 4 and 5 in this study. The overall goal in completing this listing exercise was to triangulate the data if possible, thereby making stronger connections across participants' mentoring experiences that may have not been fully realized before. Once

I completed these three columns, I sorted them into larger categories or themes (e.g., intersections of gender and mentoring) that framed or emerged from my research questions.

This analysis exercise helped me build the results chapters by using the grouped claims as outlines, and then elaborating on the connections between my research on mentoring and the work of previous researchers in writing studies. In total, I developed over 200 claims that could be supported with primary and secondary data. Chapters 4 and 5 identify two of these claims—that mentoring is a mode of learning for HealthTech employees, and that mentoring is useful in building sustainable workplace relationships at HealthTech.

All eight HTI participants expressed that mentoring is one part of their professional development "tool box," and that writing and other forms of communication (e.g., talking to one another in the hallway or during meetings) factored into at least some part of their experiences with mentoring. Other professional development practices included continuing education classes, topic-specific training seminars, and participation in research studies. Almost all HTI participants defined their workplace mentoring relationships as both "work" and "not-work," as something that is done in a workspace and may be required or strongly encouraged, and yet, almost simultaneously does not feel obligatory. I suspected that participants' experiences of mentoring as both "work" and "not-work" are because mentoring and professional development networks are often multiple, layered, and invisible. And yet, these networks are often made visible only when they are required to be, like during written performance evaluations, emails corresponding about mentoring meetings, and even social get-togethers. Still, regardless of the invisibility or visibility of mentoring at HealthTech, mentoring requires intentional, active actions. The idea that mentoring happens unexpectedly is not entirely accurate and is certainly not helpful for building productive, sustainable workplace relationships and on-demand learning. I show in Chapters 4 and 5 that mentoring is deeply connected to how HTI employees identify their genders and learning processes while at home and at work. This point is central to understanding investment mentoring as a situated and embodied rhetorical practice.

Mentoring Can Be Located, Observed, and Invented

Mentoring has long been considered a useful and often necessary part of an individual's professional development in the workplace. However, mentoring has less been considered rhetorical work—a set of strategic rhetorical practices that can assist in career-long learning—that can be observed, recorded, and analyzed for its impact on learning.

Mentoring is less assumed to be an active and critical component of an individual's ability to learn over the duration of their career, and more assumed to be necessary for certain minority groups' success or simply not needed at all. This limited understanding of mentoring can negatively affect the productive approaches to writing and learning in school and non-school settings. In this chapter, a plan for locating and observing mentoring was presented that takes seriously the rigor of undertaking such an extensive and important research topic. The methods for understanding current mentoring practices and inventing new ones prioritizes individual self-development and self-identification, and works within and across the interests of both employees and employers, and learners and teachers. In the following three chapters, mentoring as rhetorical work is more deeply considered by focusing on how HTI participants invent mentoring and the impact that has on their learning and relationship-building practices. Additionally, in Chapter 6, the mentoring experiences and stories of RCAH alumni are examined. In all, these methods can also help rhetoric and writing practitioners develop appropriate and nuanced professional development experiences aimed at student success.

Notes

1. Patrick Dias, Aviva Freedman, Peter Medway, and Anthony Pare, *Worlds Apart: Acting and Writing in Academic and Workplace Contexts* (New York: Routledge, 2013); Dorothy Winsor, *Writing Power: Communication in an Engineering Center* (Albany: SUNY Press, 2003); Jason Swarts, *Together With Technology: Writing Review, Enculturation, and Technological Mediation* (New York: Routledge, 2007).
2. Michelle F. Eble and Lynée Lewis Gaillet, *Stories of Mentoring: Theory and Praxis* (West Lafayette: Parlor Press, 2008); Pamela VanHaitsma and Steph Ceraso, "'Making It' in the Academy through Horizontal Mentoring," *Peitho* 19, no. 2 (2017).
3. JoAnne Yates, *Control Through Communication: The Rise of System in American Management* (Baltimore: Johns Hopkins University Press, 1989); Dias, *Worlds Apart.*
4. Patricia Sullivan and James E. Porter, *Opening Spaces: Writing Technologies and Critical Research Practices* (Santa Barbara: Praeger, 1997).
5. Sullivan and Porter, *Opening*, 188.
6. Sullivan and Porter, *Opening*, 188.
7. Sullivan and Porter, *Opening*, 159.
8. Liz Stanley and Sue Wise, *Breaking Out Again: Feminist Ontology and Epistemology* (New York: Routledge, 1993), 31; Jacqueline Jones Royster and Gesa Kirsch, *Feminist Rhetorical Practices: New Horizons for Rhetoric, Composition, and Literacy Studies* (Carbondale: SIU Press, 2012).
9. Stanley and Wise, *Breaking*, 157.
10. Hayden White, *The Content of the Form: Narrative Discourse and Historical Representation* (Baltimore: Johns Hopkins University Press, 1987).

11. Michel de Certeau, *The Practice of Everyday Life* (Berkeley: University of California Press, 1984); Lisa Brooks, *The Common Pot* (Minneapolis: University of Minnesota Press, 2008).

12. Thomas King, *The Truth About Stories: A Native Narrative* (Minneapolis: University of Minnesota Press, 2008).

13. Krista Ratcliffe, *Rhetorical Listening: Identification, Gender, Whiteness* (Carbondale: SIU Press, 2006).

14. Ratcliffe, *Rhetorical*, 209.

15. Ratcliffe, *Rhetorical*, 209.

16. RCAH participants did not draw mentoring network maps because of time and available resources.

17. Clay Spinuzzi, *Network: Theorizing Knowledge Work in Telecommunications* (Cambridge: Cambridge University Press, 2008), 4; Adele Clarke, *Situational Analysis: Grounded Theory After the Postmodern Turn* (New York: SAGE Publications); Brooks, *The Common Pot.*

18. Spinuzzi, *Network*, 4.

19. Eble and Lewis Gaillet, *Stories*, 309.

20. Eble and Lewis Gaillet, *Stories*, 309.

21. Doreen Massey, *Space, Place, and Gender* (Minneapolis: University of Minnesota Press, 1994); Spinuzzi, *Network*; Swarts, *Together*, 2007.

22. Clay Spinuzzi, *Topsight: A Guide to Studying, Diagnosing, and Fixing Information Flow in Organizations* (Charleston: CreateSpace, 2013).

23. Matthew B. Miles, A. Michael Huberman, and Johnny Saldaña, *Qualitative Data Analysis: A Methods Sourcebook* (New York: SAGE Publications, 2014).

24. Miles, Huberman, and Saldaña, *Qualitative.*

25. Miles, Huberman, and Saldaña, *Qualitative*, 95–99.

4 Challenging Communities of Practice

How Investment Mentoring Aids Career-Long Learning

> It's important to me to have a wide range of professional development resources available to me. Mentoring helps me, us all here at HealthTech, learn. It can be tricky, sure, but I find it's necessary.
>
> —Maria, HealthTech employee

Amy Goodburn, Donna LeCourt, and Carrie Leverenz write in the introduction of *Rewriting Success in Rhetoric and Composition Careers* that it is important for rhetoric and writing studies "to represent those alternative [professional development] narratives and, through those narratives, argue for expanding predominant definitions of professional success."[1] Taking up Goodburn, LeCourt, and Leverenz's call, this study locates mentoring as rhetorical work that can help writing studies expand current understandings of what constitutes success, not just in research, teaching, and service commitments, but also for students in the classroom and beyond. An increase in the awareness and visibility of *how* important mentoring is to the professional development of both mentee and mentor can remedy the "lack of publicly visible demonstrations of 'success'—or rather, a range of possible successes" within rhetoric and writing, the academy more broadly, and also for students who take these classes.[2] Redefining success means rethinking how to invest in the local and global work that is done in rhetoric and writing studies, and ultimately in a person's ability to learn over the duration of their career. If the attitudes of what counts as professional development and success continue to shift away from a communities of practice model, and expand to include investment mentoring, then the ways in which participation in and creation of collaborative learning for students and the field of writing studies can be more easily observed.

As I described in Chapter 2, for nearly forty years, much of the academic research and scholarship about mentoring could be described as the male experience of mentoring, which does not necessarily reflect female and/or other minority groups' experiences of mentoring.[3] In these mentoring relationships, typically two, what Chandler calls functions (i.e., outcomes) of mentoring exist, the career-enhancing function and the social one.[4] This hierarchical approach to mentoring may benefit both the mentor and mentee in particular environments and situations, especially in terms of physical safety (e.g., in research labs and on-the-job training sites). Still, in other contexts, master/apprentice practices may fail to recognize and accept the influence of the rich and complex cultural markers in the mentoring relationship, and this failure can suppress learning outcomes and growth.[5] One type of mentoring that recognizes and accepts the rich cultural identifiers in a mentoring relationship is investment mentoring. An investment approach to mentoring involves active listening, collaboration, transparency, and accessibility, and is grounded in feminist and intentionally inclusive approaches to teaching and learning.[6] Investment mentoring is committed to "justice, equality, empowerment, and peace, while keeping the contours of this notion dynamic and open, resisting the deep desire to speak as if there is no need for negotiation."[7] The brief explanation above of an investment approach to mentoring articulates a mentoring model that is broad enough that many find home in it, and it offers boundaries that are open and dynamic.

In rhetoric and writing studies, mentoring is most visible in teacher training and graduate student support programs.[8] Mentoring appears to be understood as relevant academic labor, that is, as the relationship between and/or among professors and students.[9] Still, the complexities associated with mentoring in non-traditional or alternative learning spaces (e.g., non-academic workplaces, research centers, or university writing centers), for digital and user experience, and for career-long development and professionalization, is still emerging in rhetoric and writing scholarship.[10] Current trends in existing scholarship point to the connection between professionalism and mentoring, which must include, according to Sharer, Enoch, and Glenn, "mentoring necessary for becoming a well-rounded professional, for knowing how to juggle those myriad responsibilities and expectations that accompany a faculty position."[11] Rhetoric and writing must expand current conversations that link professionalism and mentoring with teacher training to include other mentorship practices that prepare students (and even junior faculty) for their future work as researchers, teachers, and activists. Employees at HealthTech Industries (HealthTech or HTI) have experienced mentoring that is rewarding because it cultivates and expands views of professional and personal success. Their relationships span across positive, negative, and indifferent experiences, and are acknowledged as such; they are informed by the personal, historical, and cultural identity categories that each employee claims. Thus, an investment model of mentoring, one that HTI promotes, with its emphasis on intentional inclusivity and mutual empowerment, can better balance personal and professional aspects of both the mentor and mentee and support a more inclusive, participatory relationship that fosters peer-to-peer and/or career-long learning.

At HealthTech, employees use the word mentor (or mentoring, mentorship, mentoring relationship, and mentoring network) to encompass a relationship or network of two or more people with the express purpose of helping everyone involved grow intellectually, socially, and professionally. In this way, each employee involved in the mentoring relationship grows more consistently and is able to share concerns, celebrations, and achievements in a safe environment. While the ways they mentor shift based on context, available resources, and technologies, this shift also occurs because of the needs of employees at HTI, from senior employees and managers, to their many customers and clients.

Mentoring networks are often multiple, and the work of mentoring is often not positioned as scholarly work. A single network may nurture and shelter, but it also has the potential to shield mentees and mentors from scholarly and social efficiency.[12] Chapters 2 and 3 help to position this study on mentoring "as a scholarly practice," as Clary-Lemon and Roen argue, one that begins to give shape to a contextual and critical definition of how mentoring can be rightly valued in writing studies scholarship.[13] In this way, the investment mentoring model that employees at HTI advocate can help rhetoric and writing value mentoring as a scholarly practice that is inclusive, dynamic, and visible. For HealthTech employees, the "recursive dimension" or effectiveness of their investment mentoring model "is intentional . . . because it gives time for active reflection and discussion, where employees are, in some way, a part of the leading, making, and doing at HTI."[14] Investment mentoring is in line with other co-mentoring models, as mentioned above and in previous chapters.

As the stories in this chapter explain, HTI looks for project work that emphasizes their investment approach to mentoring, which supports goals of inclusion and mutual benefit. Throughout this rest of this chapter, two senior-level employees at HTI, Maria and Randall, provide examples of what investment mentoring is and how it meshes with the mission of the company. Through their examples, rhetoric and writing researchers and teachers can identify how similar mentoring practices could be adapted to different institutional contexts.

The ways HealthTech Industries supports mentoring as a mode of learning for its employees are many. Mentoring for HealthTech employees is formed out of self-directed motivations and because a person feels comfortable looking for guidance from their coworkers. An employee, feeling safe to do so, communicates what they need, and then seeks out a coworker who shares their interests, beliefs, and values, with the hopes that these similarities will help them form a mentoring relationship. This approach to mentoring and learning shifts away from Jean Lave and Etienne Wenger's communities of practice (CoP) model, and spurs on what I suggest is an investment approach to mentoring.[15] Investment mentoring promotes individual self-development and self-identification, which often leads to accessible and sustainable mentoring and workplace relationships. Additionally, investment mentoring can constitute a more appropriate and inclusive alternative to the traditional, hierarchical communities of practice model of learning. The CoP model of learning is one that rhetoric and writing studies usually endorses when classroom and workplace learning and mentoring are discussed.

HealthTech's investment approach to mentoring is part of the professional development initiatives inside and outside of the company. These initiatives are both formal and informal, and experienced daily by employees. Employees' experiences in this chapter reveal that investment mentoring supports a shift away from workplace practices that promote top-down enculturation of employees. Instead, investment mentoring positions employees as active contributors to and advocates for their mentoring needs. I end this chapter by discussing the implications and risks of an investment approach to mentoring, and the possibilities and challenges employees at HTI face when implementing, maintaining, and working within this mentoring approach. For instance, company hierarchies and employee gender, class, and age identities further complicate investment mentoring. Different kinds of mentoring can affect a person's well-being and also how they learn and advance in their careers in the present and the future.

To understand how mentoring operates at HTI, their professional development practices must be unpacked first. Mentoring, among other practices, nests itself under the larger professional development umbrella at HTI. That is, mentoring is one part of a HealthTech employee's professional development network. In addition to mentoring, other professional development opportunities exist at HTI. These opportunities range from individual and group coaching, on-the-job training, and internal and external workshops and seminars, to weekend or week-long company retreats, company meetings, lunches and dinners, and even conversations in the hallway. Collectively, these activities make up the professional development practices at HealthTech, and employees decide whether to pursue opportunities that may best help them develop personally and professionally. Maria's and Randall's stories of mentoring illustrated in the following paragraphs show how HealthTech supports the kind of rhetorical work defined earlier in this chapter and in Chapter 2, through professional development and mentoring for its employees.

Maria and Randall are senior-level employees at HealthTech, they work in different departments, and value professional development for both career and personal growth. Maria says of professional development at HealthTech,

> Professional development is having the availability of opportunities to improve [my] skills and knowledge. It [professional development] can be formal, like classes, seminars, meetings, or it can be informal, like conversations in the hallway where you don't really realize you're about to learn something.[16]

Maria continued by saying that professional development often includes mentoring and that mentoring at HealthTech "could be one-on-one or as a group, and sometimes with an awareness that it's happening and sometimes not. It can be deliberate or unintentional, [and] sometimes it's structured and sometimes it isn't."[17] For Maria, this type of professional development, or investment mentoring, is self-sought, collaborative, and accessible.

Lave and Wenger note that most people assume learning is an individual task, that it is confined in a particular time and place, and that it results from only expert instruction.[18] On the contrary, Lave and Wenger note that learning happens collaboratively and socially, and while time and place are indeed important to learning, an individual's ability to learn is not tied to one place over another or in a specific moment in time.[19] At HTI, employees facilitate their learning by distributing information and knowledge to and among fellow coworkers through scheduled meetings, emails, and conversations in the hallway or in the lunchroom area. This workplace network, composed of common workplace interactions (such as going to meetings and sending and responding to emails), builds a community of support. Employees participate in kind of discoverability or workplace findability, where they work to connect the dots between wayfinding, professional development, and self-organization and legitimization—that is, between *what* they know at work and *how* they communicate what they know to coworkers and customers.[20]

For Lave and Wenger, a site of social and collaborative learning is known as a community of practice (CoP).[21] As a group, a CoP can be found anywhere and everywhere, and participation in a CoP happens in a variety of ways, whether at work, at home, or in other social and professional spaces. Communities of practice are not new trends; this type of learning has existed for as long as people have been using storytelling to share their experiences with one another. And while communities of practice do exist at HTI, the *mentoring* relationships employees engage in rarely follow a CoP model. At HTI, employees pull apart and question Lave and Wenger's CoP model of learning in the workplace as it applies to mentoring. Analyzing the ways in which HTI employees mentor one another can make clearer why a CoP approach to mentoring can be exclusionary, and how a CoP approach to mentoring is tied to larger and arguably more problematic rhetorical performances of race, gender, class, and age.

Similarly to Maria, Randall reflected on professional development and mentoring initiatives that are part of HealthTech's career support network for its employees. For Randall, professional development is "acquiring new skills and new knowledge that enhance career performance," and it may lead to career advancement.[22] Randall continued by noting that professional development is a combination of personal, job-specific, and company-wide development activities. Randall believes that mentoring, which is a crucial part of his professional development, should be identified as such "so it can be comprehensive and sustainable."[23] The sustainability of mentoring, as Randall pointed out later, requires commitment from the mentor, the mentee, and other people who are part of an individual's network (e.g., spouses, significant others, supervisors, community leaders, and customers). Randall believes that HealthTech encourages its mentoring initiatives through planning committees, emails, written print memos, and word of mouth.[24] The significant instances of mentoring at HTI form around mentoring that happens both inside the physical structure of the company and outside of it.

Lave and Wenger might assume that HealthTech employees are part of many CoPs at work and in other social spheres, and they would be right. While a CoP is dependent on expertise, a CoP involves much more than technical know-how or skill associated with completing a task. A CoP is a group of people who are active practitioners of their craft; they come together because of a shared passion for a particular task or activity, and part of that passion is capturing tacit knowledge and increasing workplace performance and productivity.[25] In turn, people in the CoP learn to do their tasks more effectively because of their regular interactions with one another. Members of a community of practice are involved in relationships over time with other members of that CoP, and thus a community forms around the things (e.g., values, policies, programs, beliefs, activities) that matter to them *and* depend on their expertise.[26] Further, Wenger contends that CoPs are important sites of negotiation, learning, meaning-making, and identity formation.[27] And yet, the existence of a community of practice may not be evident to its members because, as Wenger continues "a community of practice need not be reified as such in the discourse of its participants."[28] In fact, it was only after the transcription, review, and discussion of their interviews that Maria and Randall learned what a CoP was. With this new knowledge of what a CoP was, Maria reflected on a professional development group, a CoP, that she was a part of at HealthTech. This group played an important part in her growth as a manager within the company. She says,

> We have a lot of homegrown managers here . . . and [years ago] my management team and I decided to meet every other Friday for development time. We went through different books [in order] to grow individually and together as a group. It was understood in this group that you could share whatever you needed to. There were even times when you got to understand better how somebody else thought of you as a manager, which really helped.[29]

Maria's CoP is not only grounded in shared ideas, shared commitments, and shared goals, but also requires expertise in a given area, and a desire to further legitimate oneself in that particular area.

Lave and Wenger note that full participants involved in a community of practice develop ways of being and doing that become established and recognized by other members of that particular group.[30] In Maria's example above, for instance, each member understood that the group formed and was sustained because each employee wanted to become a better manager. So, to accomplish their goals of becoming better managers (and therefore potentially improving the productivity of their units), they met bi-monthly to discuss ways to improve their management skills, to reflect on their own strengths and limitations as HTI employees, and to offer professional development advice for others in the group. Put another way, Maria's group of managers came together because they identified a need based on professional and shared values and concerns, and then created an opportunity, a CoP, for growth and development. Indeed, as Maria illustrates, CoPs are used as a knowledge facilitation and management practice, which is quite common in many workplaces and higher education institutions today.

Still, while CoPs are useful for an individual's professional development, Lave and Wenger do not address fully the marginalization and/or misuse of power in CoPs, and a CoPs failure to take into account learned customs and normed social codes.[31] To situate this concern further, a significant and problematic point in Lave and Wenger's communities of practice model is the idea of legitimate peripheral participation (LPP). According to Lave and Wenger, these LPP moments,

> [Provide] a way to speak about relations between newcomers and old-timers, and about activities, identities, artifacts, and communities of knowledge and practice [that form] the process of becoming a full participant in a socio-cultural practice. They also [suggest] that there are multiple, varied, more-or-less engaged and inclusive ways of being, located in the fields of participation defined by a community . . . and

when it is enabled, suggests an opening, a way of gaining access to sources for understanding through growing involvement.[32]

These moments are deliberately created or influenced, and approved and recognized by the community of practice, and are tangential to the core practices of the larger organization or company. It is understood, then, that within a community of practice, as time goes on, the newer members of the group (those who are on the periphery) will become more like old-timers (those who are central to the group's mission and function). The expectation is that, while experiencing LPP, newcomers will acquire concepts and language required to be in full communion with the CoP; the use of these concepts, language patterns, and activities require newcomers to interact with more seasoned participants, as well as with their peers. And here is where the CoP model of learning is dangerous in explaining traditional and alternative ways of learning—expectation versus reality. For now though, the focus will only be on how a CoP model for career-long mentoring is especially troublesome.

According to the *Oxford English Dictionary*, a periphery is the "marginal or secondary position in; or part or aspect of a group, subject, or sphere of activity."[33] With this definition in mind, communities of practice and legitimate peripheral participation are not only selective, but also exclusionary. The risk associated with LPP is that it is designed, possibly, to keep newcomers at the edge or periphery. The LPP is not merely an opening, or a way of gaining access to sources for understanding through growing involvement in the CoP. Rather, LPP moments can be an isolating space that grants newcomers full participation in the community of practice if—*and only if*—they adapt into the group through learning its acceptable customs and practices.

Legitimate peripheral participation can be detrimental to an individual's ability to learn over the duration of their career, especially if a CoP model is used as the *only* model for mentoring and learning. Certainly, a different workplace or context may prove LPP as less troublesome (e.g., LPP can provide physical safety to a less-experienced worker). Still, in both the best and worst case scenarios, these marginalizing dynamics exist. One has to wonder, then, what causes new members to join the CoP and why others leave it.

Peers Helping Peers: The Zone of Proximal Development and Mentoring at HealthTech Industries

Lev Vygotsky writes that the zone of proximal development (ZPD) is,

The distance between the actual developmental level as determined by independent problem solving and the level of potential development as determined through problem solving under adult guidance, or in *collaboration with more capable peers*.[34]

(emphasis mine)

Randall shares a story that clarifies the ZPD, specifically telling how he came to be a mentor for a new employee, Jack, at HealthTech. Randall says,

> There's a young man here, Jack, who's been with us for a while. I've seen Jack doing things, mostly the character he exhibits in his daily work routines that makes me want to invest my time and energy in him, to mentor him. Jack's the guy who stops in my office at 6:00a.m. with a cup of coffee [for me] and says, "Hey, Randall, I saw your light on." He's not supposed to be to work until 7:30a.m., but he shows up at 6:00a.m. with a cup of coffee and says, "Hey, I saw your light on." The heck he did see my light on! It's those kinds of people, those are the ones who I want to make an investment in, the ones who are mature, exhibit character you know. It's not so much what he did, like it's his thinking. We're similar in those ways. And so I [make time for Jack], even early in the morning.[35]

Randall's story supports mentoring that is self-sought, collaborative, and accessible. What is unique about this interaction, however, is that Jack's potential for career growth and promotion at HTI involves more than his technical skill, ability, and a willingness to adjust or adapt his beliefs and values to belong—it also involves the help or guidance of another employee, or a more capable peer, who, in a sense, is learning right beside and because of his coworker.[36] Randall and Jack have developed their own "mentoring relationship," as Randall calls it, one that is defined by giving and receiving guidance.[37] Their relationship, Randall continues, is as flattened and non-hierarchical as can be in a complex work environment; because of the company culture, rooted in long-term, strategic relationships and not only the bottom line, both men can succeed at whatever they pursue and stay committed to their goals.

At the time of this study, Randall and Jack were continuing to develop a collection of resources that they shared with one another, and with other peers who may join their network. Their collection of resources includes past and present personal and professional experiences, stories, tools and other material resources, and ways of addressing recurring dilemmas—in short, an invested practice developed and shared out of individual personal motivations. Since mentoring requires purposeful and mutually beneficial interactions, rhetoric and writing teachers and researchers must continue closely examining the relationship among how a person learns in a given context, the kind of mentoring they may receive, and the added value they contribute to their work or learning environment.

Continuing Randall's story about Jack, three spaces of personal and professional development exist for Jack in his work environment (see Figure 4.1). In the first space, Jack cannot accomplish the tasks or goals assigned to that job. For example, since Jack is a design engineer, he works in one of HTI's engineering departments. And because he works in engineering, he is not able to and does not have the expertise and interest in, for instance, writing and implementing company-wide human resources documents. Next, the second space, or the ZPD, is where Jack can only accomplish the tasks or goals in that space with the assistance of another person. If Jack wants a promotion in his department, one way to facilitate this advancement is to seek out, even briefly, supportive guidance from his network of more capable peers. And lastly, the third space is where Jack does what he was hired to do—to develop ideas, systems for manufacturing, and to improve the performance and efficiency of existing products. In this space, Jack completes tasks and meets goals that rely most heavily on his manual expertise, with little to no guidance needed

Figure 4.1 Representation of What the New Employee Can and Cannot Do with or without Help

from Randall or other peers at HealthTech. Figure 4.1 is an example of peer-to-peer learning, and Jack's ZPD.

Peer-to-peer learning can help Jack advance within HealthTech, if he desires promotion. And it can be assumed, too, that since Randall has been significant in helping Jack in one or more situations at HTI, at some point later in their relationship, Jack will help Randall with a new task or goal. Randall's ZPD and Jack's ZPD is where their investment mentoring relationship begins to take shape and matter most. In this way, investment mentoring challenges institutional and disciplinary norms, and it can empower Randall and Jack to support their collaboration and mutual success.

Investment Instead of Enculturation: An Investment Approach to Mentoring at HealthTech Industries

HealthTech participants' experiences of professional development indicate that several different kinds of opportunities for growth are available to them at work. And one of the most salient professional development practices at HTI is mentoring. An employee's investment in and motive for mentoring (as mentor and/or mentee) can now be mapped; their mentoring can be traced, linked to, and literally drawn on to their personal motivations or goals (e.g., "I want to be more active in my church community." or "I want to become a better mother."), and then extended to their professional sphere (e.g., "I want to get promoted within the next year." or "I want to learn how to listen to my coworkers better."). This mapping makes clear any gaps in knowledge an employee may have, and it also highlights the people, places, and things that are most valued in an individual's network. What was of most significance to participants was how seemingly unrelated certain tasks, people, or situations were, and how, in fact, deeply connected to one another they were. HTI employees commented that with the help of any number of mentors, they can invest in the kinds of guidance they identify as necessary for a particular situation or to accomplish a certain goal.

Randall's mentoring relationships start because of a kind of threshold or tipping point, which is something that he identifies as being an opportunity for investment.[38] These tipping points, as Randall describes them, are often small, are "felt on the inside" first, and are the motivation for seeking a mentor.[39] They may manifest as formal or informal, but most importantly these smaller moments and their outwardly expression *must* be supported by all HTI employees—the whole company culture—regardless of their participation in a particular mentoring initiative. Investing in oneself can turn into investing in others, as Randall continues, and can eventually lead to satisfactory and sustainable workplace relationships.

Both informal and formal mentoring directly contributes to the quality of the products produced and delivered by HealthTech to their customers. This investment approach to mentoring, which is explained in Chapter 2 and earlier in this chapter, can position colleagues as peers, which differs from a CoP model of mentoring that marginalizes the most at the benefit of the few. To reiterate, an investment approach to mentoring, as opposed to a mentoring approach that assumes or mandates what employees need and/ or want from professional development, positions the employee (as mentor or mentee) as capable of deciding what is best for them in a particular relationship or situation. Indeed, this contextualized approach to mentoring shifts from conformity, or a kind of workplace assimilation, to investment, or a kind of workplace parity. An investment approach to mentoring at HTI privileges all employees' learning over rigid organizational structures that put the needs of the workplace (as a product-driven manufacturing company) above the needs of its employees. This reorientation for HealthTech means that employees cannot only locate existing instances of and opportunities for mentoring, but also invent and sustain new and positive mentoring experiences within their work environment.

Investment mentoring is made up of formal and informal activities, and it is experienced by employees while at HealthTech and outside of it. Formal instances of mentoring at HealthTech are useful for employees, and they shared that they would miss the formal programs and activities were those programs to be missing from HealthTech's professional development repertoire. Still, the informal mentoring moments over lunch, coffee breaks, and hallway conversations are equally if not more important for their professional and personal growth. These informal and sometimes invisible moments occur because of the daily, ordinary work practices of employees. The ability to mentor and/or be mentored in the here-and-now, as Maria emphasizes, is "directly connected to timely and accurate shipment of product to customers now and in the future."[40] In short, employee learning and their relationships with one another directly correlate to customer and client satisfaction.

Maria understands investment mentoring at HealthTech as "generative and cyclical, from the top to the bottom, or the bottom to the top, and around again."[41] To illustrate, Maria says that because her boss participates in positive mentoring relationships, he then encourages her to find mentoring opportunities that best suit her needs. And, as might be assumed, she in turn encourages those within her unit to seek mentoring opportunities that make the most sense for them. She recalls,

I've learned by example to make time for, to take the time out of my day-to-day routine, to do mundane, simple things, like making time for opportunities and learning, like scheduling seminars, scheduling to [take] a class or even walking down the hallway to grab a pop and learn something from a coworker I see or pass by.[42]

Formal and informal professional development investments point again to McGuire and Reger's idea of co-mentoring, and at HTI, the mentoring initiatives between and among employees in the same or different divisions occur frequently within the company.[43] One reason co-mentoring initiatives are possible at HealthTech is because of professional development organizations outside of HealthTech that work with employees in finding and working with a mentor or mentee. These external opportunities, for instance, provide HealthTech employees with valuable material resources, as well as networks of other business and medical professionals.

An Investment Approach to Mentoring at HealthTech Industries: A Case Example

HTI employees have the option to participate in an organization outside of the company whose mission it is to support, mentor, and develop executive, managerial, and production-level professionals in the Midwest. This case example focuses primarily on the Midwest organization as a whole, as well as a specific mentoring initiative in which many HTI employees are involved. This Midwest organization supports a model of professional development that promotes consistent interaction and learning, which enables all members to perform roles and tasks safely with low risk. This organization, no doubt, further supports an investment approach to mentoring at HTI.[44]

HealthTech is a part of a Midwestern nonprofit organization, or as employees call it a learners' group, which was founded a few years ago by business professionals in the region.[45] The organization is dedicated to supporting the professional interests of women and men in the Midwest by inspiring, supporting, and empowering them to achieve personal and career success. The organization offers educational opportunities to its members in the form of workshops, invited speakers, and group and one-on-one mentoring. These opportunities build individual leadership skills and business connections, and support mentoring relationships between and among members.[46] Being part of the organization offers many tangible and/or material benefits, including the following:

- connecting with other professionals in the Midwest,
- building a cross-industry network of engaged professionals,
- developing knowledge and leadership skills through organization-sponsored programs and events,
- supporting mentoring through a separate mentoring program,

- volunteering in regional and local communities, and
- honing professional skills by being part of the organization's many committees and/or board of directors.[47]

Additionally, the organization promotes many other benefits, such as being associated with a leading organization and being recognized for one's professional and/or career-advancing accomplishments. As of June 2014, the organization had over ten corporate sponsors to assist with event planning and event implementation, and to help with the total financial stability of the organization.[48]

The organization holds many events throughout the year and makes available additional material resources to its members. Past events have included how to build one's personal and professional brand, how to take full advantage of one's strengths for personal and professional growth, and speed networking with other business professionals.[49] The organization also offers print and online resources like documents/print texts, handbooks, website links, online webinars, video links, and other downloadable materials to its members.[50] This information can be used for continued and sustained personal and professional development across time and space.

Perhaps most interesting to this case example is that the Midwest professional development organization has a mentoring program available to its members.[51] While there is a modest registration fee for the program (to help offset the costs of materials and events), HTI employees find the mentoring program to be beneficial to both mentees and mentors. And, according to documents from the mentoring program, the following lists reflect these benefits to both mentees and mentors respectively:

For Mentees

- develop strengths and overcome weaknesses,
- develop new skills and knowledge, and
- create career and professional development plans.

For Mentors

- help others reach their maximum potential,
- be recognized as an expert and leader in the organization and in their field,
- gain exposure to fresh perspectives, ideas, and approaches, and
- develop and sharpen their leadership and coaching style.[52]

A person can serve as both a mentor and mentee (e.g., several employees at HTI have been both a mentee and a mentor while part of the program, sometimes simultaneously), and mentees have access to one-on-one and/

or group mentoring.[53] Other mentoring activities and resources include monthly mentoring meetings, meet-and-greet events (where mentor/mentee pairings and/or groupings take place), and facilitation tools (like guide books, workbooks, and online and print resources). As a member of the mentoring program, an individual must participate in monthly self-initiated mentoring sessions, and all associated program events.[54]

The minimum amount of time a mentor devotes to the mentoring program is one hour a month, and they are required to help with at least three organization events during the year. The minimum amount of time a mentee devotes to the mentoring program is one hour a month, plus any planning and follow-up activities of which no specific amount of time is indicated.[55] Mentors are also required to attend three organization events during the year. While a mentee and their mentor usually attend the same events during the year, mentees and mentors are not required to attend the same events together.[56]

Before HealthTech committed to sponsoring the organization's mission and mentoring program, Maria and another female colleague were "approached [by the CEO of HealthTech] [to do] some experiential research, and see if [the organization] was something that HealthTech needed."[57] So, Maria and the other female colleague asked the Midwest organization's board of directors to attend one of the organization's events free of charge, so they could observe and interact with other members of the organization. The board agreed, and plans were made for Maria and her coworker to attend the upcoming event. Still, even after plans were solidified, Maria recalls that she was hesitant to attend the event. For Maria, previous professional development and mentoring experiences that were particularly unhelpful heavily influenced her willingness to participate in other and future development initiatives.[58]

Still, HTI decided to join the organization, and employees at HealthTech have found it appropriate to their development needs. Since joining the Midwest organization seven years ago, the employees at HealthTech have reaped many benefits as members, and as mentors and mentees. Maria says,

> It's been a very rewarding experience since I can go outside my comfort zone to be mentored by different people. So, by connecting with a bigger group of people, and bringing in ideas from multiple facets, because you have so many people from different industries who are part of this organization, it expands my reach in being able to give and receive support like this, and to help maintain a program like this. Being part of it has really helped me professionally, mostly because I surround myself with people who share their life experiences inside and outside of work.[59]

HTI employees' experiences with the Midwest organization have been largely positive. Because HealthTech's approach to business focuses on building lasting relationships between and among employees and with customers, the help from this professional development organization enables HealthTech to continue to support its employees. The professional development opportunities available to employees can lead to better quality products, and happy and satisfied customers. Additionally, these development opportunities give employees, as Randall notes, avenues "to talk to smart people, [and] to take advantage of those opportunities where we can find a mentor or two."[60] This regional organization is a needed and supported addition to HealthTech's investment approach to mentoring because its impact on the employees at HTI reaches not only their home or personal lives, but also the many people with whom they do business. The implications and risks of investment mentoring raise a few important questions about mentoring as a mode of learning not only for HealthTech Industries, but also for rhetoric and writing practice.

Formal and informal mentoring are generative in allowing mentors and mentees time to meet and discuss issues of professional and personal interest.[61] And Maria illustrates that her experiences with mentoring and other professional development activities have been mostly useful for her. At HTI, employees, both new and old, can talk about personal and professional goals, ranging from family planning and self-esteem building, to workplace promotions and building their professional networks. Whether formal or informal, mentoring is most successful when it consists of reciprocal, self-aware, and transparent peer-to-peer learning.

For Randall, Amaury Nora and Gloria Crisp's four mentoring constructs are upheld in both formal and informal mentoring instances that occur inside and/or outside of HealthTech.[62] Nora and Crisp posited that the most positive and productive mentoring relationships adhere to four principles:

1. psychological and emotional support,
2. support for setting goals and choosing a career path,
3. subject knowledge support aimed at advancing a learner's knowledge relevant to his or her chosen field, and
4. the specification of a role model.[63]

It can be concluded that Randall's past experiences with mentoring, whether positive or negative, heavily influence his approach to mentoring Jack.

Interestingly, what emerged from HTI participant interviews were two additional constructs not proposed by Nora and Crisp: *mentee willingness and mentor/mentee predisposition to mentoring*.[64] A mentee's willingness to participate in and support a culture of mentoring depends in large part on the mentee's previous perceptions and/or experiences with mentoring. Jim Henry, Holly Huff Bruland, and Jennifer Sano-Franchini write that "the presence of a mentee is a self-evident necessity for mentoring, [but] the degrees of engagement" for the mentee can vary significantly.[65] Limited mentee engagement or even refusal to participate in the mentoring relationship or its activities, for instance, often leads to unnecessary stress for both the mentor and mentee. Randall and Jack, for example, continue to have a productive mentoring relationship because of Jack's willingness and initiative to seek out Randall. Moreover, this study illustrated the impact previous mentoring has on employees' current mentoring relationships, and how these predispositions shift over the course of their mentoring at HTI. In the next chapter, I show how gender identity affects mentoring and employees' work performances because of it. In the end, investment mentoring at HTI can be beneficial to all employees involved, and has far-reaching, positive implications for local community members and customers as well.

While formal mentoring is a vital part of non-academic workplaces and academic institutions across the country, as Maria and Randall have shown, informal mentoring often happens alongside and as an extension of formal mentoring.[66] Informal mentoring relationships are fruitful in allowing mentors and mentees to meet and discuss issues of professional and personal interest when and how it's convenient for them; however, a distinguishing characteristic between formal and informal mentoring is that the informal relationship is often characterized by mentors and mentees coming together because of shared and/or similar personal interests, personality types, and even friendship. For Randall especially, the informal support he gave and continues to give and receive from Jack has allowed their relationship to evolve toward a more co-equal one, despite Randall having worked at HTI longer than Jack. At HTI, mentoring often happens when employees least expect it, and as Maria notes, "that's pretty darn cool."[67] Mentoring occurs in a multitude of spaces and places, and with many and varied tools and technologies. In some ways, too, mentoring is also used to subvert and rebuild existing social and ideological structures within the company to allow for more and better opportunities of collaboration and inclusion.

In Chapter 5, I focus on the idea that mentoring is rhetorical work that builds relationships, and I detail how an HTI employee's gender identity is connected to their ability to opt out of mentoring. The cost of opting out of or non-participation in mentoring is higher for some HTI employees than it is for others. While HealthTech supports an investment approach to mentoring, some employees (e.g., women and other minorities) have to work harder at investing than do others. If all HTI employees are not willing to participate in investment mentoring supported by the company, then access to guidance and resources can disappear. Therefore, employees may receive mixed messages about the value of mentoring and other professional development practices within the company.

Notes

1. Amy Goodburn, Donna LeCourt, and Carrie Leverenz, "Introduction," *Rewriting Success in Rhetoric and Composition Careers*, eds. Amy Goodburn, Donna LeCourt, and Carrie Leverenz (Anderson: Parlor Press, 2013), ix–x.
2. Goodburn, LeCourt, and Leverenz, *Rewriting*, xviii.
3. Christy Chandler, "Mentoring Women in Academia: Reevaluating the Traditional Model," *NWSA Journal* 8, no. 3 (1996): 79.
4. Chandler, "Mentoring."
5. Gail Y. Okawa, "Diving for Pearls: Mentoring as Cultural and Activist Practice Among Academics of Color," *College Composition and Communication* 53, no. 3 (February 2002).
6. Gail McGuire and Jo Reger, "Feminist Co-Mentoring: A Model for Academic Professional Development," *NWSA Journal* 15, no. 1 (2003); Jacqueline Jones Royster and Gesa Kirsch, *Feminist Rhetorical Practices: New Horizons for Rhetoric, Composition, and Literacy Studies* (Carbondale: SIU Press, 2012); Patricia Sullivan, Michele Simmons, Kristen Moore, Lisa Meloncon, and Liza Potts, "Intentionally Recursive: A Participatory Model for Mentoring," *Proceedings of the 33rd Annual International Conference on the Design of Communication* (July 2015).
7. Jones Royster and Kirsch, *Feminist*, 644.
8. Sally Barr Ebest, "Mentoring: Past, Present, and Future," in *Preparing College Teachers of Writing: Histories, Theories, Programs, and Practices*, eds. Betty Pytlik and Sarah Liggett (New York: Oxford University Press, 2002).
9. Scott Miller, Brenda Jo Bruegemann, Bennis Blue, and Deneen M. Shepherd, "Present Perfect," *College Composition and Communication* 48, no. 3 (1997); Lynn Bloom, "Mentoring as Mosaic: Life as Guerilla Theater," *Composition Studies* 35, no. 2 (2007); Ken Baake, Stephen A. Bernhardt, Eve R. Brumberger, Katherine Durack, Bruce Farmer, Julie Dyke Ford, Thomas Hager, Robert Kramer, Lorelei Ortiz, and Carolyn Vickery, "Mentorship, Collegiality, and Friendship: Making Our Mark as Professionals," in *Stories of Mentoring: Theory & Praxis*, eds. Lynee Lewis Gaillet and Michelle F. Eble (West Lafayette: Parlor Press, 2008); Jennifer Clary-Lemon and Duane Roen, "Webs of Mentoring in Graduate School," in *Stories of Mentoring: Theory & Praxis*, eds. Lynee Lewis Gaillet and Michelle F. Eble (West Lafayette: Parlor Press, 2008).
10. Kristine Blair, Angela Haas, and Christine Tulley, "Mentors Versus Masters: Women's and Girls' Narratives of (Re)Negotiation in Web-Based Writing Spaces," *Computers and Composition* 19 (2002); Sullivan, Simmons, Moore, Meloncon, and Potts, "Intentionally Recursive"; Heather Noel Turner, Minh-Tam Nguyen, Beth Keller, Donnie Johnson Sackey, Jim Ridolfo, Stacey Pigg, Benjamin Lauren, Liza Potts, Bill Hart-Davidson, and Jeff Grabill, "WIDE Research Center as Incubator for Graduate Student Experience," *Journal of Technical Writing and Communication* 47, no. 2 (March 2017).
11. Wendy Sharer, Jessica Enoch, and Cheryl Glenn, "Performing Professionalism: On Mentoring and Being Mentored," in *Stories of Mentoring: Theory & Praxis*,

eds. Lynee Lewis Gaillet and Michelle F. Eble (West Lafayette: Parlor Press, 2008), 129.

12. Bloom, "Mentoring"; Clary-Lemon and Roen, "Webs."
13. Clary-Lemon and Roen, "Webs," 178.
14. Sullivan, Simmons, Moore, Meloncon, and Potts, "Intentionally," 7.
15. Jean Lave and Etienne Wenger, *Situated Learning: Legitimate Peripheral Participation* (Cambridge: Cambridge University Press, 1991).
16. Pseudonym used to protect identity; Maria, in discussion with the author, February 2014.
17. Maria, interview.
18. Lave and Wenger, *Situated*.
19. Lave and Wenger, *Situated*.
20. Peter Morville, *Ambient Findability* (Sebastopol: O'Reilly, 2005); Malea Powell, Daisy Levy, Andrew Riley-Mukavetz, Marilee Brooks-Gillies, Maria Novotny, and Jennifer Fisch-Ferguson, "Our Story Begins Here: Constellating Cultural Rhetorics," *Enculturation: A Journal of Rhetoric, Writing, and Cultures* (2014).
21. Lave and Wenger, *Situated*.
22. Pseudonym used to protect identity; Randall, in discussion with the author, February 2014.
23. Randall, interview.
24. Randall, interview.
25. Lave and Wenger, *Situated*.
26. Lave and Wenger, *Situated*, 98.
27. Etienne Wenger, *Communities of Practice: Learning, Meaning, and Identity* (Cambridge: Cambridge University Press, 2000).
28. Wenger, *Communities*, 125.
29. Maria, interview.
30. Lave and Wenger, *Situated*.
31. Alessia Contu and Hugh Willmott, "Re-embedding Situatedness: The Importance of Power Relations in Learning Theory," *Tamara: Journal of Critical Postmodern Organization Science* 14, no. 3 (2003); Stephen Fox, "Communities of Practice, Foucault and Actor Network Theory," *Journal of Management Studies* 37, no. 6 (2000); Allistair Mutch, "Communities of Practice and Habitus: A Critique," *Organization Studies* 24, no. 3 (2003).
32. Lave and Wenger, *Situated*, 29, 36–37.
33. Oxford Online Dictionary, "Periphery," accessed May 20, 2018, https://en.oxforddictionaries.com/definition/periphery.
34. Lev Vygotsky, *Mind in Society: The Development of Higher Psychological Processes* (Cambridge: Harvard University Press, 1978), 86.
35. Randall, interview.
36. Vygotsky, *Mind*, 68; Bill Hart-Davidson, "Learning Many-to-Many: The Best Case for Writing in Digital Environments," in *Invasion of the MOOCs: The Promises and Perils of Massive Open Online Courses* eds. Steven D. Krause and Charles Lowe (Anderson: Parlor Press, 2014).
37. Randall, interview.
38. Randall, interview.
39. Randall, interview.
40. Maria, interview.

41. Maria, interview.
42. Maria, interview.
43. McGuire and Reger, "Feminist."
44. Maria, interview.
45. Pseudonym used to protect identity; Maria, interview.
46. Maria, interview.
47. Maria, interview.
48. Maria, interview.
49. Maria, interview.
50. Maria, interview.
51. Maria, interview.
52. Maria, interview.
53. Maria, interview.
54. Maria, interview.
55. Maria, interview.
56. Maria, interview.
57. Maria, interview.
58. Maria, interview.
59. Maria, interview.
60. Randall, interview.
61. Carol Berkenkotter, Thomas N. Huckin, and John Ackerman, "Conventions, Conversations, and the Writer: Case Study of a Student in a Rhetoric Ph.D. Program," *Research in the Teaching of English* 22, no. 1 (1988); Barr Ebest, "Mentoring"; Rebecca Rickly and Susanmarie Harrington, "Feminist Approaches to Mentoring Teaching Assistants: Conflict, Power, and Collaboration," in *Preparing College Teachers of Writing: Histories, Theories, Programs, and Practices*, eds. Betty Pytlik and Sarah Liggett (New York: Oxford University Press, 2002); Janice Lauer, Michele Comstock, Baotong Gu, William Hart-Davidson, Thomas Moriarty, Tim Peeples, Larissa Reuer, and Michael Zerbe, "Their Stories of Mentoring: Multiple Perspective on Mentoring," in *Stories of Mentoring: Theory & Praxis*, eds. Lynee Lewis Gaillet and Michelle F. Eble (West Lafayette: Parlor Press, 2008).
62. Amaury Nora and Gloria Crisp, "Mentoring Students: Conceptualizing and Validating the Multi-dimensions of a Support System," *Journal of College Student Retention: Research, Theory and Practice* 9, no. 3 (2007).
63. Nora and Crisp, "Mentoring," 340; the author has not analyzed Nora and Crisp's four constructs in relation to a CoP model of mentoring; however, such work should be done.
64. A similar construct was also observed in Henry, Huff Bruland, and Sano-Franchini's 2010 article in the *International Journal of Teaching and Learning in Higher Education* about class-attached mentoring, first-year writing, and academic support.
65. James Henry, Holly Huff Bruland, and Jennifer Sano-Franchini, "Educating Reflexive Practitioners: Casting Graduate Teaching Assistants as Mentors in First-Year Classrooms," *International Journal of Teaching and Learning in Higher Education* 22, no. 3 (2010): 315.
66. Chandler, "Mentoring"; Cindy Moore, "A Letter to Graduate Student Women on Mentoring," *Profession* (2000); Kendall Leon and Stacey Pigg, "Graduate Students Professionalizing in Digital Time/Space: A View From 'Down Below',"

Computers and Composition 28 (2011); Amy C. Kimme Hea and Melinda Turnley, "Managed Care: All-Terrain Mentoring and the 'Good Enough' Feminist WPA," in *Performing Feminism and Administration in Rhetoric and Composition,* eds. Krista Ratcliffe and Rebecca Rickly (New York: Hampton Press, January 2010).
67. Maria, interview.

5 Investment Mentoring Is Rhetorical Work That Builds Relationships

> I knew an employee here needed work, needed development, needed mentoring. She says she wants to be mentored, but sometimes I think she doesn't want to hear the truth, face her past. I know that one priority is getting product out the door, and that's very important, but there's more to it than that. And I tell her "I'm an open door, I'm going to stop what I'm doing and I will meet with you." I guess, it's about looking in the mirror every day, saying, "I'm a great person, I love this person I see." Because, at the end of day, it's about understanding your core self, and how you feel about you.
>
> —Julie, HealthTech employee

In Chapter 4, I illustrated mentoring as a process that is made up of self-directed motivations or investments by the employees at HealthTech Industries (HealthTech or HTI). An HTI employee, feeling comfortable to do so, articulates what they want or need, and then they seek out a coworker who shares their personal and professional interests, beliefs, and values. This approach to mentoring and learning shifts away from Lave and Wenger's communities of practice model and prompts an investment mentoring model.[1] This new approach to mentoring promotes individual self-development and self-identification, which can lead to accessible and sustainable mentoring and work relationships for employees.

Eble and Lewis Gaillet write in the introduction of *Stories of Mentoring* that the book's primary purpose is to "define the current status of mentoring" in rhetoric and writing studies by giving "insight into the character of those rare individuals who embody the term mentor."[2] They note that the stories found in the book are temporally and situationally bound, and each story offers different conceptions of mentoring as students and teachers within English studies experience it. And while each chapter provides a different view of how mentoring is enacted, the stories offer, according to the Eble and Lewis Gaillet, "effective models of mentoring," while providing "heuristics for building mentoring programs that view mentoring as a scholarly activity."[3]

As I stated in the introduction, the strategies, anecdotes, and experiences about mentoring in the edited collection do not seek to provide a definition of mentoring per se, but rather glimpses into the professional and personal relationships that constitute academic institutions, departments, and programs. Academic mentoring, writes Eble in the conclusion of the book, assumes many forms including but not limited to "co-teaching [and] dissertation directing . . . advising . . . and modeling effective administrative and professional activities."[4] *Stories of Mentoring* is representative of particular moments in time, and is not exhaustive of all kinds, models, and situations of mentoring.

Mentoring, when done well, is mutually beneficial for and respectful toward all persons involved. However, too often, mentoring is not reciprocal nor is it respectful, and "resistance to mentoring exists and power/authority struggles are real."[5] A close examination of power and authority struggles in a particular work environment reveals how exactly mentoring can and should continue to matter to rhetoric and writing practice. To illustrate, Dorothy Winsor examines how engineers and engineering students learn to write in an organization, and how they navigate the organization's many workplace networks.[6] Winsor argues that writing does more than communicate knowledge: it generates new knowledge, trains new knowledge creators and workers, and can support the organization's hierarchical power structure. In a similar way, Winsor's analysis and explanation of the relationship between writing and power is useful when understanding how mentoring, like writing, can also support or challenge an organization's workplace structure. And as Katherine Miles and Rebecca Burnett note, it is when the "little things" of mentoring like gender identity are explored, that the sometimes hidden social motives of the workplace are exposed.[7] Certainly, as I show in this chapter, a person's gender identity is not a "little thing," but rather can be indicative of how mentoring is more or less a distributed, workplace activity.[8]

Therefore, citing James Sosnoski and Beth Burmester, Eble and Lewis Gaillet challenge rhetoric and writing studies to continue to rethink the colonial master/apprentice models of mentoring where "apprenticeship helped maintain the distance between masters and apprentices, in the conditions of their labor and wages."[9] They call for future research on mentoring to "focus on fostering mentoring relationships that occur across boundaries of race, ethnicity, class, gender, sexuality, and disability," that is, research that acknowledges, contextualizes, and even celebrates identity differences, while encouraging mutual benefit and respect between/among mentors and mentees.[10]

With their challenge in mind, I focus this chapter on how mentoring is rhetorical work that can build workplace relationships, and how an individual's gender identity complicates these relationships, access to mentoring, and the sustainability of it. Specifically, I argue that mentoring, like an individual's gender identity, has a performative dimension to it. Throughout this chapter, women's experiences of mentoring, or mentoring experiences that involve women at HTI are discussed and analyzed. Their stories are the focus of this chapter because the women in this study (particularly the participants from HealthTech) identified their gender identities as affecting their mentoring relationships. What is more, many of the women interviewed in this study indicated that their gender identity and mentoring relationships intersect in ways that cannot only put their mentoring relationships at risk but also their jobs. I end this chapter by beginning to answer Jeffrey Jablonski's charge to writing studies to create and work with "professionalizing strategies [that] are appropriate in career contexts."[11] In discussing the appropriate professionalizing strategies put forth by Jablonski, I extend his argument to consider the cost(s) of non-participation in mentoring and other professionalizing relationships.

To reiterate from Chapter 2, I define and use feminism and gender identity by calling on Jones Royster and Kirsch, borrowing their definition of feminism as the "commitment to justice, equality, empowerment, and peace, while keeping the contours of this notion dynamic and open, resisting the deep desire to speak as if there is no need for negotiation."[12] This chapter illustrates that HTI employees' stories of mentoring make space for open and dynamic understandings of gender identity, professionalism, and the rhetorical work that builds and maintains these relationships.

Additionally, I draw on Judith Butler's idea of performativity to inform how participants' gender identities are discussed throughout the chapter.[13] To be clear, in this chapter and elsewhere, I am not using the word *performativity*; rather, I articulate the *performative dimension* of an employee's gender as it is socially constructed and shaped by relations of power. The ways a HealthTech employee identifies their gender, and/or is identified by their gender are multiple, complex, and contribute to the sustainability of mentoring within the company. Additionally, I show in this chapter that not every HTI employee acknowledges that gender positively or negatively influences mentoring.

The people in this study identified as female or male, as man or woman, and as gay or straight. Additionally, HTI and RCAH participants referred to themselves as male and man, as female and woman, and/or as a mother or father, with no distinction or separation between their sex, gender, or associated roles and responsibilities. For the scope of this chapter, I use their self-identifications within the context of their interviews to analyze their mentoring experiences. There is no intentional implication of any further meaning(s) about their gender identities or identifications.

How Gender Identity Complicates Investment Mentoring at HTI

> I don't think my gender affects the way I mentor others at HealthTech. When it comes to mentoring women, I think there's a sensitivity side to mentoring them, and being able to understand that sensitivity side may impact how I mentor [women at HealthTech]. But, I try to treat everybody the same way. And yeah, sometimes I don't get the sensitivity side of [mentoring women]. [And if I need help], I ask a female coworker to help me. So, I guess, I don't see gender as a big deal.[14]

Patrick, above, is a senior-level employee at HTI and identifies as a straight man and father.[15] He has worked for HealthTech for several years, and in his department the majority of employees with whom he works are men. Patrick's experience illustrates an all-too-familiar attitude when it comes to mentoring and professional development between and among gender differences—that, especially in male-dominated industries like engineering or manufacturing, certain kinds of identities are more common and can be more acceptable than others. And as such, he does not need to see "gender as a big deal," because his gender identity is likely part of the dominant structures that his discipline (i.e., engineering) identifies as normal. It can be assumed, then, that his approach to mentoring may be similar and can result in him either asking a female coworker for help in mentoring (which is not necessarily a bad thing but can result in more work for his female colleague), or, as he later clarified during his interview, opting out of difficult or "sensitive" mentoring situations altogether.[16] His experience of mentoring women is not to be dismissed; it highlights that his gender identity is most likely considered standard, normal, or typical at HealthTech.

In Chapter 4, I suggested that mentoring helps HTI employees learn not only a skill or trade but also helps them learn about the beliefs and values that make up their work environment. Collin Craig and Staci Perryman-Clark point out that a workplace culture most certainly is complicated by gender identity. They write that all institutional structures, which would include HealthTech, have "particular investitures around identity that align relations of power to representation."[17] Further, they suggest, certain identity categories like those that represent race (e.g., white or Caucasian) and gender identity (e.g., man and male) align more easily with top-down, power structures and ideologies. Following their thread, Patrick's story indicates that, because he can more easily align his identity with existing company structures, he can also keep his gender identity separate from his mentoring relationships and work responsibilities. This separation can allow him to opt out of these "sensitive" mentoring situations because, as he understands it, "gender isn't a big deal."[18] Patrick's gender affords him the privilege to choose which relationships he is a part of, and which he is not, with minimal cost to his workplace reputation. To be sure, Patrick should be accountable to everyone with whom he works; however, he is not to be solely blamed for the disciplining structures that make up his discipline. His story illuminates how an individual HTI employee can opt in or out of professional development initiatives for any number of reasons with little to no cost to their job or professional status.

I previously stated in this chapter and in Chapter 4 that women employees at HTI experience mentoring and their genders as deeply connected. In addition to the Midwest organization discussed in Chapter 4, women employees at HTI were, at one time, associated with a different national organization committed to providing women in biotechnology with opportunities to develop professionally in their work environments. Maria, speaking for herself and other women employees too, remembers that the national organization,

> Just wasn't the right fit. The women on that board, they're good people and all, really, but they wear suits to work every day, and we, uh, don't. Everything we did [for professional development and mentoring] had to be approved by them, which was also approved or, sort of, in line, like by [our] corporate structure. [The national mentoring group] was like being part of another business.[19]

Maria's gender identity is closely tied to what she wears to work. That is, for Maria, wearing suits to work indicates a more rigid enculturating approach to work, which could be a sign of other professional development activities like mentoring. And because of Maria's and others' experiences with the national organization, HealthTech's involvement with them did not last much more than a year. Once again, it is clear that mentoring is affected by the personal, social, and ideological motivations of both an individual and a workplace.

Moreover, Claire, another senior-level employee at HealthTech, says that her gender identity influences not only how she performs her roles as mentor and/or mentee, but also the ways in which others expect her to perform her gender, her work tasks, and mentoring roles at HealthTech. To explain, Claire is an active and contributing member of the Midwest professional development organization discussed in Chapter 4, and she spends much of her time within the organization growing the mentoring program. Still, because of Claire's gender identity and sexual orientation, and self-identification as a gay woman (both in personal and professional spaces), she frequently wonders how her gender identity and sexual orientation affect how others value her as a mentor and/or mentee. She recalls,

> The Midwest organization, they wanted me to come and help them out [with their mentoring program]. I [was] like, "Well, what if these ladies find out about me and they don't want me there because I might not be the right kind of . . . what's the word I want . . . role model for them." I guess I worried about how my coming out would affect things, whether it would be directly here at HealthTech or out in the larger community. I was afraid that I would be a blemish on HealthTech, or that the ladies in the [Midwest organization] would find out about me, if they didn't already know, and [say] "You can't be in this group. We're trying to be good examples for people."[20]

Claire's experience above illustrates that her gender identity is intimately connected to her experiences with work and mentoring. She worries (almost constantly) that how she performs her gender identity and sexual orientation will make it difficult for her to get the mentoring she needs for personal and professional development.[21] And, unlike Patrick, it can be supposed that Claire's gender identity might not be considered normal in her professional development environments. Claire might be seen as, according to her, "too different or too difficult to work with" by the Midwest organization, and therefore directly or indirectly encouraged to leave the group.[22] Luckily for her, this has not been the case, and she remains active with the organization today.

Claire states that the intersections of her gender identity, sexual orientation, and mentoring helps her educate others at work and in the community about acceptance and accountability. She says,

> Going back to my personal experience [of identifying as a gay woman], there were and still are opportunities I have to be an example to people. There's this huge dynamic [in coming out], and I finally just had to let the negativity go and say, "I hope I can make a difference, and that if there are people in the [Midwest organization] [who] have an issue with me, that I can change their mind." I want them to think "you're one of us, and you're here for the same reason as we are. To learn."[23]

Patrick's, Maria's, and Claire's mentoring stories show that gendered bodies operate within a matrix of power, which is often invisible and can be confusing to navigate. How mentors and mentees use their gender identity to mark themselves and others in the workplace can factor into how mentoring happens because, as Craig and Perryman-Clark write, "our beliefs that how one identifies racially, politically, or by gender gauges literacy practices, and how one shapes relationships with others."[24] Therefore, the ways Patrick, Maria, and Claire engage with others at HTI and in the Midwest professional development organization are dependent on two criteria:

1. how they understand their own gender identities, and
2. how they interpret others' genders as a signification of and expectation for how mentoring should happen between themselves and others at work and in the community.

The performative dimension of gender identity is crucial in understanding professional development and mentoring; depending on how an employee's gender is enacted, they and others at HTI may receive mixed messages about the value of mentoring and other practices within the company. The complexities associated with gender identity in traditional mentoring relationships are often not acknowledged or recognized as valuable attributes to its goals and outcomes. Failure to identify, recognize, and accept the influence of gender identity in the mentoring relationship not only suppresses desired learning outcomes and growth for both the mentor and mentee, but also quickly shifts the focus of the relationship to the unspoken or ignored intricacies of mentoring.

The matrix of power that restricts certain gendered bodies and influences workplace mentoring relationships is, according to Rebecca Rickly, manifested most significantly as the "old boy's network."[25] The old boy's network approach to mentoring is often associated with master/apprentice models of advising and guiding, and other practices that foster hierarchical and patriarchal ways of navigating institutional settings. In this way, mentoring is a disciplining mechanism, one that keeps certain people in (straight, male, man) and others out (straight, gay, female, woman). And yet, while women and other minorities are usually not welcomed in these more traditional old boy's networks, they often do not desire these types of exclusive, competition-driven relationships in the first place. Rather, as this chapter makes clear, women usually (but not always) prefer to devote their time, talent, and energy to mentoring relationships that are mutually and inclusively supportive and productive. These kinds of relationships "avoid the problems associated with the traditional model, withstand the stress of career interruptions and family responsibilities," and promote inclusive learning for both mentor and mentee.[26] Investment mentoring has the potential to do just this—to acknowledge an individual's gender identity as significant to and an essential part of mentoring and learning.

All too often, however, as Cindy Moore points out, women experience poor and even personally and professionally hurtful mentoring or no mentoring whatsoever.[27] Poor mentoring or a lack of mentoring can occur because of unequal distribution of material resources, a lack of respect for both the mentor and mentee, and even personal differences like not being friends.[28] The mentoring experiences throughout this study, and in this chapter specifically, reveal that a communities of practice approach to mentoring thrives off of exclusion rather than inclusion; a mentor or mentee not acknowledging or accepting the nuances of one another's genders can be a reason for the mentee not becoming or being allowed to be a full participant in the mentoring community.

For some women employees at HTI, informal mentoring relationships are more easily flattened or non-hierarchical, are more likely to be positive, and can lead to personal and professional satisfaction and even career growth. An informal mentoring relationship is often characterized by mentors and mentees coming together because of shared or similar personal interests (i.e., not necessarily work related) and personality types (e.g., introversion or extraversion).[29] These informal mentoring relationships often focus on relationship building, by placing an equal focus on the ways two or more people are connected to each other as well as the objective goals of mentoring like career advancement. These informal mentoring relationships are crucial to helping an individual transition into new work roles as professional collaborators, with the emphasis on developing productive and lasting relationships as colleagues.[30]

Baake et al. provide a useful starting point for understanding the importance of building a mentoring relationship around shared interests, personality traits, and even friendship, yet what they fail to address completely is the significance an individual's gender identity in not only developing a mentoring relationship, but also sustaining it. Julie at HTI discusses an informal mentoring experience she had as a member of a community-wide women's group. Julie explains,

> I've always been involved in women's groups both [associated with HealthTech] and outside of work. [These] groups are fun; a lot of [them] are about networking and even mentoring, and a lot of the women in [these] groups are also professionals, or teachers, or executives. I also belong to two [informal] groups of girls' night out, one from here at work and one outside [of work]. And to some degree, we're all friends who are all professionals. For us, it's about networking and just spending time [outside of work] together. But personally, for me, it's about keeping my friends and common interests close, which I think is also crucial for mentoring.[31]

The relationships Julie fosters with women both at work and in other social and professional arenas are mostly positive and critical for her personal and professional growth. And she relies on and values informal opportunities to make up her mentoring network and experiences. Her relationships are built on shared personal interests and experiences, and these shared qualities are found at work, at home, and in her hobbies (e.g., one of the groups Julie belongs to a group of women who are dedicated to fun, fitness, friendship, and leading an overall fulfilling life). Julie is not required by her supervisor at HTI to attend any of these formal and informal mentoring activities; rather, she seeks out these moments because she believes they are vital to her growth as a woman and as a professional. In Chapters 2 and 3, I detailed the feminist and relational investment model of mentoring used in this study that "seeks to dispel the view of the disembodied intellectual by attending to [an individual's] familial, personal, and emotional needs," all of which, as I have shown, affect mentoring and its professional and personal goals and outcomes.[32] And, from Julie's story, HealthTech employees value a kind of co-mentoring that "emphasiz[es] the importance of cooperative, non-hierarchical relationships for learning and development."[33] Through their transparent conversations and the company's values of relationships and respect first (not to be confused with employees' disagreement), HTI employees make explicit the need to take seriously how their gender identity impacts mentoring. Because of this, several of the mentoring initiatives at HTI are ones of investment and not enculturation.

Julie's story more clearly depicts how an investment approach to mentoring at HTI is enacted. An investment approach to mentoring supports— indeed it *insists* upon—that the mentor and mentee seriously consider and value the relationship they are about to enter together. Mentors and mentees must regularly talk about, write, and/or draw or map out the expectations of their relationship. Moreover, an investment approach to mentoring acknowledges and attends to the practices and positionalities held in common (or not) by the mentor and mentee. In Julie's story, a co-mentoring relationship, with its emphasis on mutual empowerment, makes her not only feel safe in learning and growing as a woman and professional, but also helps her create safe spaces for other similar women to, in her words, "see if there's anyone out there, who [they] can relate to."[34]

And while many female employees at HTI value relationship building and attendance to shared interests and practices in their mentoring endeavors, some women at HTI are invested in mentoring that encourages masculinist values of hierarchy and competition. Consequently, Julie's story does not speak for all women at HealthTech. Vertical advancement within a workplace and even lateral promotion are risky for women, especially when management and executive-level positions are occupied by women who are or were willingly a part of the old boy's network. To illustrate, Maria talks openly about her mentoring experiences with women at HTI and in other professional spaces that were not useful to her. Unlike Julie,

some of Maria's mentoring experiences with other women were more negative than positive.

According to Maria, women, more than men, tend to hold on to personal
and professional bitterness in the workplace, which can lead to an uncomfortable and, at times, hostile work environment. In Maria's view, some
women in professional spaces are "two-faced" in their approach to helping
other women succeed.[35] Maria recalls a specific instance of mentoring, outside of HTI yet connected to it where "somewhere [in our smaller group],
the breakdown of the group had to do with some of the other women. Like I
said before, you know how women can be together. We hold on to grudges
more than men do."[36] While mentoring can be a useful and necessary way to
build and sustain her relationships at work, Maria recognizes that mentoring
can also create an aggressive tension between the women in her professional network. This tension is often encouraged by intense competition for
attention from and recognition by peers and supervisors, and also highly
coveted resources like the newest technology and also time off. Maria further clarifies her mentoring experience by saying,

> [This] hypocritical thing goes on. "Hey, you want to get together? Want
> to grow together?" And we do grow together, but only in certain 'rah-
> rah' spaces. And sure, [some of us] eventually have a support group at
> HealthTech. Yet others, who claim to be all about mentoring, walk by
> my office everyday, and the least [they] could do is say "hi" or "how's
> it going?" since they see me sitting there, but they don't. They just keep
> on walking.[37]

Maria's story shows that the who, the when, and the where of mentoring
are also an integral part of an investment approach to mentoring for Health-
Tech employees. The who, the when, and the where of mentoring can come
with a hefty price, as is seen previously in this chapter. For women at HTI,
the price of being "one of the boys" is often a willingness to turn against
other women colleagues, especially if maintaining the workplace status quo
means job security.

The tendency to compete with one another further marginalizes women's
access to support and information, and even continued informal and formal
mentoring opportunities. What is often viewed as "just workplace cattiness
between women" can be the first step toward the breakdown of workplace
communication and productivity. Therefore, while mentoring in one space
can be considered safe and conducive to learning, in another space mentoring presents a kind of threat to an individual's professional relevancy. And
because the risk—perceived or actual—associated with career advancement for women is lived daily for most women, mentoring relationships

that traverse professional spaces and places are sometimes tricky at best and the cause for workplace insecurity and paranoia at worst.

So far in this chapter, I have articulated that workplace mentoring relationships can be positive and negative, informal and formal, and most of all, they can be the nexus by which career advancement can happen. A person's gender identity cannot only complicate the mentoring expectations of both mentor and mentee, but also the kind of career advancement options available to the mentor or mentee. Gender expression is fluid and flexible, and not mandatory and rigid; so, too, can a person's job description with myriad tasks and activities that make up their work routine. Advancement or promotion within a particular department or workplace, for example, can be tied to company values and expectations, and not necessarily performing a job-specific duty satisfactorily or even exceptionally well. When examining how career advancement happens, leading career studies theorist Michael Arthur notes that teachers and researchers must,

> Move beyond seeing careers as artifacts of any single organization. Instead, our interest must lie in how careers are linked to the founding, discovery, evolution, learning, networking, and alliance-building of organizations.[38]

Contemporary careers are not tied to specific worksites or institutions. While careers may be located in a particular workplace (e.g., HealthTech), the work that employees do travels across organizational lines; their very careers can be viewed as boundaryless.[39] In a similar way, mentoring can also be understood as boundaryless, and that an individual's experiences of mentoring traverse the physical structures of a particular workspace.

Over the last thirty years, many workplaces have evolved into environments that are marked by highly skilled knowledge workers, workers who produce information (through writing and conversations) as separate from other material goods.[40] This more open and inclusive understanding of work has replaced the normative view of an individual's career as a stable and lifelong commitment. A boundaryless career, similarly to mentoring, can be one full of possibility, opportunity, transitions, and higher career satisfaction. However, these types of careers can also be ripe with uncertainty and instability.

While the kinds of work and the types of careers most present today are not the focus of this study, these accurate depictions of what work is like can help highlight how mentoring aids career-long learning. The development of a boundaryless career depends on an individual's relationships with colleagues and friends, and with professional organizations and personal connections. The ability of mentoring to build productive and mutually beneficial relationships can be, as Jeffrey Jablonski suggests, an appropriate strategy for navigating today's fluid or boundaryless work environment.[41] Jablonski writes that writing studies research and teaching focuses on writing as a spatially and temporally situated activity, which severely limits the possibilities of the writer and their writing. This way of understanding writing potentially "overlooks fundamental shifts in our global economy and the behavior of workers."[42] Rhetoric and writing must shift their intra-organizational perspectives to inter-organizational ones, notes Jablonski, perspectives that closely examine individual and group career practices that may shape larger societal ways of being and doing.[43]

These individual and group career practices, as HTI employees have illustrated, include all kinds of professional development practices that can lead to or support an investment approach to mentoring. Earlier in this study, employees talked about how mentoring at HTI feels both like "work" and "not work," and often at the same time. In other words, because certain aspects of their careers are boundaryless, HTI employees can construct investment mentoring for and with one another that is not directly tied to company hierarchies. This way, they can make more obvious the social actions and expectations within their workspaces that, in turn, can inform their career trajectories.

And yet, what a career studies perspective on learning and mentoring does not fully address is how an individual's work performance and gender identity are either in sync or in interference with one another. Some of Maria's experiences with workplace mentoring have been less than ideal, and yet her stories raise an important consideration for rhetoric and writing practitioners. If mentoring happens, according to Maria, "inside this [particular space] but not outside of it" and if "we are all supposed to be the same, in this equal group" then what's at stake for:[44]

1. an employee's access to the kinds of mentoring they need in order to learn over the duration of their career, and
2. women and other minorities to mentor and be mentored in ways that are most appropriate and effective for them.

Patrick's, Maria's, Claire's, and Julie's stories point to an important cultural shift within the company, a shift that takes seriously the need for an investment approach to mentoring to help mediate the intersections of work, mentoring, and gender identity at HealthTech.

The Costs of Non-participation in Mentoring Initiatives at HTI

I end this chapter by briefly highlighting of some of the costs of non-participation in mentoring for employees at HTI. Each potential case of non-participation plays an important role in making visible the cultural shift HealthTech employees may experience addressed at the end of the previous section in this chapter.

> What I mean is, guys have to be open to women being able to be successful. Some men here just don't do it . . . well, there's still that mentality [here at HealthTech] of guys being better than we are. And even if they are asked to be a mentor [to a woman], they [men] might come into it with kind of a poor attitude about it because they aren't really invested in growing, but more about who's better than who [sic]. And that's not really mentoring, not good mentoring anyways.[45]

Claire observes that her male coworkers can more easily opt out of mentoring at HealthTech. And their opting out is linked to their assumptions about their female coworkers' abilities to be successful in their jobs at HTI. Additionally, she illustrates that for some employees at HealthTech, building and investing in sustainable relationships is not necessarily a top priority. And failure to build productive relationships can cause employees not only to resent one another, but also to be cautious of or refuse any or all professional development opportunities at HealthTech, including but not limited to mentoring. What can result, then, is a kind of workplace loneliness, which has been shown in many of Maria's and Claire's mentoring experiences and workplace stories.

Maria's experiences show writing studies teachers and researchers that learning is collaborative and collective. Maria's story in Chapter 4 about not finding the right kind of mentor for her illustrates that some of Nora and Crisp's mentoring constructs were broken.[46] Maria believes she did not receive the personal and professional support she needed for setting and achieving goals, nor was she able to find a role model. And she takes ownership of her refusal to participate in some of the mentoring at HTI.[47] Still, while mentee willingness is indeed crucial for the sustainability of mentoring, it is also clear that for Maria, a fifth mentoring construct manifested in her participation in investment mentoring: *mentor willingness*. Maria recalls that not finding a role model was not for lack of trying; she remembers several instances of seeking out a mentor only to find colleagues who were "too busy."[48]

Moreover, as with other company-wide practices and policies at Health-Tech, the implementation and sustainability of mentoring initiatives across multiple physical locations of a company can be tricky to do, especially since the work at HTI can span multiple physical locations and can be invisible to customers and colleagues alike. The recent growth and global expansion of HTI, for instance, makes it difficult to not only provide consistent mentoring programs for employees, but also ensure that the mentoring that does happen can be measured. Maria reflects on this issue, saying "one of the problems that I've seen going through [HealthTech] is as the company has gotten bigger, [we've] just gotten so focused on growing the company that those development opportunities have become less important."[49] Similarly, Randall talks about the difficulty of making mentoring sustainable at HTI, saying "the size of HealthTech is what makes professional development and mentoring hard to maintain" but also noting that because the sustainability of mentoring is difficult to achieve, does not mean trying to sustain it should not be a goal that is regularly attempted.[50] Certainly, the size of HTI impacts the supportability of mentoring; however, Maria, Claire, and even Patrick prove that ignoring or dismissing an employee's gender identity affects the access to and longevity of mentoring more than the size of the company.

HealthTech employees' stories of mentoring predict that when one person or even a group of people ignore or reject the shared beliefs and goals of mentoring at HTI, the ties in the larger network (e.g., the Midwest professional development organization, the outside mentoring program) have the potential to break or fade away. As a result, an employee's access to guidance and resources can disappear, because it is assumed that the advice from more capable peers is no longer needed, wanted, or valued. In short, if HTI employees are not willing to acknowledge and/or participate in investment mentoring initiatives supported by the company, then employees may receive mixed messages about the value of mentoring and other professional development practices within the company.

It is no surprise that Patrick, Maria, Claire, and Julie experience mentoring in vastly different ways. And the professional needs of women HTI employees and the assumptions made by men HTI employees about their colleagues' needs must be addressed through contextually appropriate mentoring models. While it is imperative to remember that Patrick, Maria, Claire, and Julie are, in some way, "bound" to their careers (as evidenced by their job titles and routine work duties), all four employees are knowledge workers and require careers that are flexible and adaptable, careers that allow for personal interruptions, travel time, and experiential learning.[51] Put another way, investment mentoring can help HTI employees, especially Maria, Claire, and Julie, locate their individual needs, scaffold those needs alongside HealthTech's organizational goals, and determine if they are adding value to themselves, their career, and the company. Their experiences and practices, in turn, can hopefully help Patrick interrogate his privilege and the ways he understands professional development at HealthTech.

Mentoring is just one way for HTI employees to build and sustain relationships both inside and outside of the company. And the stories that framed this chapter revealed that an employee's gender identity affects the investment approach to mentoring at HTI discussed in previous chapters in both positive and negative ways. This chapter prioritized HTI employees' stories and experiences of mentoring as each experience is connected to their gender identity.

During and after individual interviews and focus groups with HTI employees, they reflected on just how complicated and difficult it is to sustain mentoring. Their experiences of mentoring almost always included a mention of or reference to how they performed their genders or were expected to perform their genders either at home or at work. It was not surprising, then, that many of the women HTI employees interviewed for this study talked extensively about their gender identity affecting their workplace relationships, including their mentoring relationships with other men and especially other women at the company.

Still, while no male employee talked explicitly about being mentored by a female employee, the male employees' stories show that gender identity is a factor that contributes to how they mentor or have been mentored in the past. An employee's gender identity is connected to their ability to opt out of mentoring, and the cost of opting out or non-participation is higher for some employees than it is for others.

In Chapter 6, the focus of the book shifts slightly from mentoring HTI employees to mentoring college students who were part of a residential college at Michigan State University. Chapter 6 discusses the types of learning and mentoring activities RCAH participants experienced while in school and their experiences of mentoring at work. Because of RCAH participants' stories, I argue that rhetoric and writing teachers are best able to teach mentoring as a rhetorical practice that acts as a powerful means to professional success inside and out of the university. To continue building value in rhetoric and writing research, writing studies practitioners must re-evaluate their commitments to positive, sustainable relationship-building practices. Investment mentoring constitutes a more appropriate and sustainable alternative to the hierarchical communities of practice model that rhetoric and writing so readily accepts when school and non-school learning is discussed.

Notes

1. Jean Lave and Etienne Wenger, *Situated Learning: Legitimate Peripheral Participation* (Cambridge: Cambridge University Press, 1991).
2. Michelle F. Eble and Lynée Lewis Gaillet, *Stories of Mentoring: Theory and Praxis* (West Lafayette: Parlor Press, 2008), 3.
3. Eble and Lewis Gaillet, *Stories*, 306.
4. Elbe and Lewis Gaillet, *Stories*, 307.
5. Eble and Lewis Gaillet, *Stories*, 309.
6. Dorothy Winsor, *Writing Power: Communication in an Engineering Center* (Albany: State University of New York Press, 2003).

7. Katherine S. Miles and Rebecca E. Burnett, "The Minutia of Mentorships: Reflections About Professional Development," in *Stories of Mentoring: Theory & Praxis*, eds. Lynee Gaillet and Michelle F. Eble (West Lafayette: Parlor Press, 2008), 127.

8. William Hart-Davidson, Clay Spinuzzi, and Mark Zachary, "Visualizing Writing Activity as Knowledge Work," *Proceedings of the 24th Annual International Conference on Design of Communication* (Myrtle Beach, SC, 2006).

9. James Sosnoski and Beth Burmester, "New Scripts for Rhetorical Education: Alternative Learning Environments and the Master/Apprentice Model," in *Culture Shock and the Practice of Profession: Training the Next Wave in Rhetoric and Composition*, eds. Virginia Anderson and Susan Romano (New York: Hampton Press, 2005); Eble and Lewis Gaillet, *Stories*, 6.

10. Eble and Lew Gaillet, *Stories*, 309.

11. Jeffrey Jablonski, "Seeing Technical Communication From a Career Perspective: The Implications of Career Theory for Technical Communication theory, Practice, and Curriculum Design," *Journal of Business and Technical Communication* 19 (2005): 37.

12. Jacqueline Jones Royster and Gesa Kirsch, *Feminist Rhetorical Practices: New Horizons for Rhetoric, Composition, and Literacy Studies* (Carbondale: SIU Press, 2012), 644.

13. Judith Butler, *Gender Trouble: Feminism and the Subversion of Identity* (New York: Routledge, 2006).

14. Pseudonym used to protect identity; Patrick, in discussion with the author, February 2014.

15. I do not analyze Patrick's identification as father in this chapter; however, the intersections of mentoring, gender identity, and parenting are worthy of future study.

16. Patrick, interview.

17. Collin Craig and Staci Perryman-Clark, "Troubling the Boundaries: (De)Constructing WPA Boundaries at the Intersections of Race and Gender," *WPA* 34, no. 2 (Spring 2011): 39.

18. Patrick, interview.

19. Maria, in discussion with the author, February 2014.

20. Claire, in discussion with the author, February 2014.

21. Claire, interview.

22. Claire, interview.

23. Claire, interview.

24. Craig and Perryman-Clark, "Troubling," 38.

25. Rebecca Rickly, "Mentoring, (Wo)Mentoring, and Helping Students Take Responsibility for Their Own Education," *Kairos* 5, no. 2 (2000): 2.

26. Christy Chandler, "Mentoring Women in Academia: Reevaluating the Traditional Model," *NWSA Journal* 8, no. 3 (1996): 94.

27. Cindy Moore, "A Letter to Graduate Student Women on Mentoring," *Profession* (2000): 149.

28. Moore, "A Letter," 150.

29. Ken Baake, Stephen A. Bernhardt, Eve R. Brumberger, Katherine Durack, Bruce Farmer, Julie Dyke Ford, Thomas Hager, Robert Kramer, Lorelei Ortiz, and Carolyn Vickery, "Mentorship, Collegiality, and Friendship: Making Our Mark as Professionals," in *Stories of Mentoring: Theory & Praxis*, eds. Lynee Lewis Gaillet and Michelle F. Eble (West Lafayette: Parlor Press, 2008).

30. Baake, Bernhardt, Brumberger, Durack, Farmer, Dyke Ford, Hager, Kramer, Ortiz, and Vickery, "Mentorship," 65.
31. Julie, in discussion with the author, February 2014.
32. Gail McGuire and Jo Reger, "Feminist Co-Mentoring: A Model for Academic Professional Development," *NWSA Journal* 15, no. 1 (2003): 54.
33. McGuire and Reger, "Feminist," 57.
34. Julie, interview.
35. Maria, interview.
36. Maria, interview.
37. Maria, interview.
38. Michael Arthur, "The Boundaryless Career: A New Perspective for Organizational Inquiry," *Journal of Organizational Behavior* 15 (1994): 297.
39. Arthur, "The Boundaryless"; Michael Arthur and Denise Rousseau, *The Boundaryless Career: A New Employment Principle for a New Organizational Era* (Oxford: Oxford University Press, 1996); Sherry Sullivan and Michael Arthur, "The Evolution of the Boundaryless Career Concept: Examining Physical and Psychological Mobility," *Journal of Vocational Behavior* 69, no. 1 (2006); Svenja Tams and Michael Arthur, "New Directions for Boundaryless Careers: Agency and Interdependence in a Changing World," *Journal of Organizational Behavior* 31, no. 5 (2010).
40. Arthur, "The Boundaryless," 297–298; Johndan Johnson-Eilola, *Datacloud: Toward A New Theory of Online Work* (New York: Hampton Press, 2005); William Hart-Davidson and Jeffrey Grabill, "Understanding and Supporting Knowledge Work in Schools, Workplaces, and Public Life," in *Writing in Knowledge Societies*, eds. Doreen Starke-Meyerring, Anthony Paré, Natasha Artemeva, Miriam Horne, and Larissa Yousoubova (Fort Collins: WAC Clearinghouse, 2011); Thomas Barker, "How to Teach Career Planning Beyond the Next Job," *Intercom* (2013).
41. Jablonski, "Seeing."
42. Jablonski, "Seeing," 7.
43. Jablonski, "Seeing," 39.
44. Maria, interview.
45. Claire, interview.
46. Amaury Nora and Gloria Crisp, "Mentoring Students: Conceptualizing and Validating the Multi-dimensions of a Support System," *Journal of College Student Retention: Research, Theory and Practice* 9, no. 3 (2007).
47. Maria, interview.
48. Maria, interview.
49. Maria, interview.
50. Randall, in discussion with the author, February 2014.
51. Clay Spinuzzi, *Network: Theorizing Knowledge Work in Telecommunications* (Cambridge: Cambridge University Press, 2008).

6 Pedagogical Implications for Rhetoric and Writing Studies
Case Examples of Mentoring in a Residential College

Mentoring is a process. It's about creating a cohesive element. And I've learned it can be about the way you dress. And what language you use. About long-term and future planning. And an awareness of the community you're in. So yeah, there's definitely good mentoring and bad mentoring. I think the good mentoring is grounded in common core values, creative problem solving, and tone. The way you're addressed, verbally non-verbally, or whatever, it matters. Yeah. It's about values. Common, core values and goals. That's what mentoring is to me.

—Alex, RCAH alum

Mentoring helps build a community of scholars and ensures that knowledge building continues in each new generation.
—Michelle Eble, *Stories of Mentoring: Theory and Praxis*

The mentoring I received from RCAH faculty also caused me to question the stuff I was learning in my other classes. So, like, how is what I'm doing practical? What am I supposed to be learning from all the reading and the writing? How do these skills translate to the workplace?
—Carrie, RCAH alum

In the earlier chapters of this book, I built an inclusive framework for studying the connections among mentoring, rhetoric and writing practice, professional identity development, and experiential learning. This framework set the foundation for showing how to do a rhetorical analysis of mentoring. This study proposed a feminist and qualitative methodology for why mentoring matters to rhetoric and writing practice, and then articulated a set of methods for locating and examining how mentoring facilitates career-long learning in both academic and non-academic institutions. A good majority of these chapters focus on the mentoring experiences and stories of HTI employees because I was most curious about how mentoring happens outside of the university classroom in order to inform what can happen inside of it. As a former English major and current teacher and scholar of writing, I am most familiar with the mentoring practices that make up the various academic institutions, departments, and programs of which I was and am a part. It made sense to me, therefore, to look for other examples of mentoring that could be useful models for writing studies practice.

The focus of this chapter shifts slightly to highlight how mentoring can happen in classroom spaces, by primarily drawing on personal interviews and also rhetoric and writing scholarship that illustrate how mentoring can happen in alternative learning spaces (e.g., research labs and writing and tutoring centers), and in other academic spaces like university hallways, faculty offices, and living-learning spaces like dormitories and cafeterias.[1]

In Chapters 2 and 3, I discussed in great detail the primary research site for this study, HealthTech Industries. In this chapter, however, I explain my connection to the second site for this study, the Residential College in the Arts and Humanities (RCAH) at Michigan State University (MSU). During the 2013–2014 academic year, I was selected to be an RCAH Graduate Fellow, which required me to develop a yearlong project that looked at some aspect of the scholarship of teaching, learning, and engagement. According to the RCAH website,

> The RCAH and the Graduate School at MSU jointly sponsor a graduate fellowship program for doctoral students with interests in teaching, learning, engagement, and assessment in higher education. The primary goals of the RCAH Graduate Fellowship Program are to provide professional and career development opportunities outside of regular classroom instruction for a diverse group of graduate students as mentors, tutors, and group leaders in various aspects of the RCAH and to contribute directly to the scholarship of teaching, especially in the areas of the humanities, world language proficiency, the visual and performing arts, and civic engagement.[2]

One of several residential colleges for undergraduate students at MSU, RCAH focuses exclusively on issues that often matter most to arts and humanities students and faculty. RCAH is built on four central themes: world history, arts and culture, ethics, and engaged learning. Students live and learn in a custom-built environment that includes dorm rooms, a cafeteria, classrooms, a theater, art studio, gallery, language and media center, and music practice rooms. Their class sizes are typically small (twelve to fifteen students in a class), which can provide an intimate space for more in-depth conversations about current events and topics that interest students. Moreover, as the RCAH alumni stated during their interviews, the smaller class sizes allowed them to interact and engage with their classmates in various ways, including question-of-the-day conversations, free writing exercises, and other brainstorming activities. These learning activities often extended beyond the classroom and into their meal times and social activities.

The RCAH Graduate Fellows program is comprised of doctoral students enrolled in programs across MSU. These programs are associated with the Colleges of Arts and Letters, Music, Education, Social Science, Communication Arts and Sciences, and Agriculture and Natural Resources. The doctoral students selected for this program "participate in group meetings twice a month and smaller discussions with other fellows, outside speakers, and faculty members on topics related to teaching, learning, and engagement," and a monetary stipend is given to fellows to help them present their research findings at conferences and in peer-reviewed journals.[3] Each Graduate Fellow is required to design and execute a yearlong research project focusing on any aspect of teaching, learning, or educational assessment and build that project within the residential college. Since I was interested in mentoring and learning in academic and non-academic environments, it felt natural to expand my study to include RCAH students and/or alumni.

My first year as an RCAH Graduate Fellow in 2013–2014 coincided with the design and defense of my dissertation prospectus. In my prospectus, I articulated a study that would examine both academic and non-academic mentoring experiences, practices, and relationships. After all of the reading I had done on mentoring in academic spaces, I wondered if there was some connection between mentoring in the college classroom and mentoring in the workplace. I chose to interview recent college graduates (within two to three years from the time of interviews for this study) because I was interested to learn about any of their professional development practices that began in the residential college that may have transferred to their new work environments.

In 2013–2014, I interviewed three RCAH alumni about their mentoring experiences inside and outside of the residential college. I wanted to know how each RCAH graduate invented, located, and mobilized mentoring that was learned while a student of the college. At the time of this study, each graduate was employed full time, and they occupied various levels of leadership in their workplaces across the country. The interview questions I asked RCAH alumni were the same questions I asked HTI employees. In total, I interviewed eleven people for this project—three college graduates from RCAH at MSU, as well as eight senior-level employees from HealthTech—to see if the kind of mentoring that happened in one place happened in another, and if it did, how it contributed to alumni experiences of professional development in their new work environments. With the addition of RCAH alumni, the study developed into a multisite project, with the goal of locating, observing, and better understanding how mentoring is invented and sustained in a workplace and in an academic department or program.

This chapter extends the conversation about mentoring in non-school settings (i.e., HealthTech Industries) to include the mentoring stories and experiences shared by college graduates who were part of the RCAH at MSU. I discuss three case examples in this chapter, and each example from RCAH alumni paints a rich picture of the complexities and intersections of mentoring and learning in both school and non-school settings. While no RCAH alumni specifically addressed mentoring that happened in a writing classroom or because of explicit writing instruction (i.e., no specific writing or English course was addressed during participants' interviews), their experiences of mentoring act as yet another model that writing studies practitioners can find useful in helping students invent, use, and prioritize mentoring alongside interdisciplinary learning in any class or workplace situation.

Case Example One: Meet Alex[4]

Alex was part of the first graduating class from the RCAH at MSU in 2011. His decision to study in the residential college was an easy one; he knew he wanted to study psychology in college, but he also knew he wanted to have access to culturally situated, multidisciplinary learning experiences. It was also important to him to study at a school that had options for small class sizes and individual instruction. "I was given a lot of individual attention in the RCAH," he recalls, "And I could do what I wanted to in psychology, and I could also do this other thing, along with fifty others, and be a part of this new residential college, which allowed me to get a fair and balanced look at the world."[5]

Ever since he was a child, Alex was interested in the world around him. So, it was only natural for him to seek out learning experiences that allowed him to understand the cultures that made up the world and how he could interact with them. He recalls,

> I was able to be absorbed into the humanities through sociology, anthropology, literature, and writing. I wanted to broaden my understanding of the individual by trying to understand the sort of different levels of humanity in a whole, integrated system.[6]

And because of his thirst for knowledge, he found himself "looking for someone, anyone, to teach me how to be a better human. RCAH gave me the ability to think critically in multiple ways, how to communicate properly and from different angles with different groups of people."[7]

During his senior year of high school, and after applying to MSU for college admittance, Alex was selected to be part of the Honors College at MSU. Because of his high academic achievement in high school, he was automatically eligible to be considered for a tuition-assistance scholarship. As a result, he was awarded a Professorial Assistantship, which is awarded to MSU Honors College invitees with exceptional academic records; he received a monetary stipend for faculty-mentored research, which was renewable for four semesters (two academic years).[8] He says of the assistantship,

> I was assigned a professor to do their work with them, help them with their research work for two years. And it happened almost instantly when I started at RCAH. One day, the professor I was going to be working with saw me walking down the hallway and was all "Hey! You're my guy!" and he just threw me into work right away. Talk about mentoring.[9]

In the two years Alex worked as an RCAH professorial research assistant, he also helped develop and co-teach a series of learning and engagement forums with his assigned faculty-mentor. These forums, according to Alex, fostered an "open dialogue on important issues, bringing together students and professors from different disciplines all across the MSU community."[10] He helped teach, facilitate, and at times, mediate intense discussions about human rights, race and justice, and technology and creativity. He remembered, "I had one particular moment where I was leading a discussion and I received a lot of pushback from someone in attendance." He continued to reflect on the situation saying, "but what is most interesting about the whole thing is the professor I was teaching with didn't jump in and protect me. He trusted me, because he had already pushed me so far, knew I had a lot to learn, and he wanted to challenge me."[11] These experiences in the RCAH would go on to inform everything else Alex expected of professional development—in the residential college, in his current employment, and in his life more generally.

Even though Alex was new to teaching and research at the college level, he was given the opportunity to teach with his assigned RCAH faculty-mentor. He looks back at this experience as a turning point, saying,

> the situation I was in at the RCAH was unique, and both personal and professional. Professors invested in me as someone with certain beliefs and core values, and as someone who would eventually graduate and go on to work out there.[12]

He was not prepared for every task required or expected of him while in the RCAH, but he was willing to try.

The courses Alex took in the RCAH provided him with "connections to local and surrounding community members" where he was "able to network with like-minded folks."[13] And while the courses were impactful for him, it was the mentoring he experienced in RCAH that enabled him to take advantage of those connections in productive ways. Learning and professional development networks are not always readily visible, and as Chapter 5 makes clear, barriers exist that can prevent networks from being accessible in the first place, let alone used by individuals who seek out those networks. When I asked Alex about finding mentorship opportunities in the residential college, he noted that each professional development experience was a "happy accident of finding the right person and the right opportunities," further situating his experiences by indicating that he did not spend time intentionally building networks, but rather was encouraged to seek out a mentor or two or three should he need them.[14] However, he recalls,

> the harder I tried to get someone to mentor me, the less I got from them, meaning we weren't a good fit for any number of reasons. And maybe I wasn't really paying attention to who could best help me, but they somehow noticed me.[15]

The interest or investment in him by faculty, staff, and other students was critical in helping him find his place in college life.

The situational and contextual components of investment mentoring illustrate, as Alex points out, that "informal mentoring and formal mentoring are about layering," and for him all professional development is multiple and "woven together."[16] When understood in this way, investment mentoring is accumulated or collected over time, each separate present action affecting future actions and outcomes. Alex also noted that, for him, a significant aspect of layered professional development is made up of both the mentor and mentee understanding or at least accepting one another's "sense of humor, personality, and previous external experiences of mentoring."[17] His prior experiences of mentoring affect how he engages with his peers and superiors, not only as mentee but also as a student and future expert in his field. The "external experiences of mentoring," that Alex refers to are all of the other mentoring and professional development happenings that occurred outside of the residential college (e.g., the mentoring he received from other professors at MSU, and the mentoring relationship he had with a friend in his theater troupe).[18] These "external" experiences were actual accumulations of professional development that helped form and inform Alex's identity as a student and worker.[19] "I joined RCAH because I wanted to be part of something new and cool. I stayed because of the resources and people who made the experience and education possible."[20] Alex found RCAH to be accessible, available, and supportive.

After graduating from RCAH, Alex completed a graduate degree, and began working in his field right after graduate school. "It was a jarring experience," Alex states of his transition from school to work, mostly because "I had only known how to do school, and I did it well for a long time. I went from RCAH to graduate school to my first full time job."[21] Previously, he had internships with organizations in the East Lansing area, but nothing quite like the work that became his new normal. Alex further described his transition from full time student to full time employee as "different" and "a little unexpected" in parts, deviating from his experiences of learning and supervision in the residential college. He says of his job,

> At my new job, which was part of a really small organization, I was hired largely because I was fresh out of graduate school, and so the assumption was that I knew all of the latest techniques and could teach others what I had learned. I guess, in a way, they thought I would fit well within the forward motion of the company, within their vision.[22]

While Alex did fit with the company's mission and goals, he recalls seeking someone or a group of people from his job to help him develop professionally. He needed guidance in understanding how to do the work that was expected of him at this particular workplace, in learning and adapting to their way of work. Alex's previous mentoring experiences in RCAH were positive and productive, and he figured as much would happen in his new job. However, he found it challenging to find a mentor at work because his employer had a difficult time making mentoring available to new employees. He remembered thinking "I was always wondering if this [professional development] thing we were doing was relevant to the mission of the company."[23]

Alex continued to talk about "fit" at his job, and just how hard it was for him to find a mentor or two at work. He expressed that a person's personal ideologies and worldviews matter to and inform mentoring. "I think to myself, how can I grow in a way that positively reflects my company, but also stays true to the core principles that guide and impact my life more generally?"[24] And what happens, as Alex questions, when "directors change, and then so do the practices and experiences of work and professional development."[25] Certainly, management styles, turnover within a company, and employee productivity can dictate the creation and longevity of professional development initiatives. Moreover, employees entertain these initiatives with varying degrees of acceptance. Alex was looking for a person or group of people to help him "become better at what I'm doing in the arc of my career. If I'm better at tasks, then I'm better at communicating and interacting with people. And vice versa."[26]

As it turns out, however, the kinds and types of professional advice that Alex eventually received from his colleagues were anything but helpful. The type of feedback he received was unlike anything he had experienced before in the residential college. Looking back, he recognized these moments to be about "the outwardly minute tedium of the way I operate as an individual," noting several instances of contradictions between what he thought would matter in his job and what actually did.[27] He continued to contextualize his workplace experience by saying, "I thought what would matter would be how I interacted with clients and the work I was doing."[28] Unfortunately, he was wrong.

Earlier in Chapter 5, I suggested that mentoring is rhetorical work that builds relationships, and I discussed some of the implications about the risks of failing to acknowledge the persistently relational nature of mentoring. Alex helps to make this point even clearer by recalling,

> When I first started working here, I was told often that the way I dressed and the way I spoke was too "high" for the kind of work I was doing. Really, I didn't dress badly or anything, no ripped clothes or holes or whatever. My supervisor just wanted me to look and act a certain way when dealing with clients. The way I dressed and how I spoke didn't impact my caseload, either. I should say, though, that this is just one of her things. If my shirt was buttoned wrong, or if I wore these pants that are jean material but colored like slacks. Didn't work for her. I had to purchase a whole new wardrobe. So much focus was on how I was appearing and not the work I was doing.[29]

The ways in which expectations of professionalism factor into current and future mentoring relationships can send mixed messages to mentees—especially new employees—about the quality of their work and their ability to contribute to the reputation of the company or organization.[30] Alex recognized that how he dressed at work mattered to his identity as a professional, and that it not only impacted his supervisor's perception of him, but also colored her ability to fairly assess whether he was, as he says, a "team player." He notes, "I remember thinking, 'Am I dressing like my coworkers? Am I really too different?'"[31] These seemingly little or individual variations from what is considered normal, acceptable, or standard in a workplace can leave a person feeling overwhelmed and even marginalized (similarly to Maria's story in Chapter 5 about what she wears at work). And certainly, it is important for an individual to interrogate how they, as Alex continues, "come off" to others. Still, reciprocity, or mutual benefit, is one of the core characteristics of investment mentoring. And Alex's example illustrates that mutuality between him and his supervisor was not fully actualized. In fact, it could be concluded that his supervisor was more invested in enforcing company rules and adhering to policy about what Alex should wear than investing in Alex as a person.[32] Alex concluded our conversation by remarking, "it's easy to tell someone, to tell me, to change their appearance because, in my case, those are things my supervisor can see. She doesn't know me, like what I believe or whatever, so this is easy for her."[33] Easy, perhaps, but her advice has the potential to do long-term damage for Alex's personal and professional growth.

Case Example Two: Meet Carrie[34]

Carrie graduated from MSU in 2011 and, like Alex, was part of the first graduating class from the RCAH. After graduation, she spent several months working various jobs not directly related to what she studied in school. Eventually, Carrie found herself working for the MSU College Advising Corps, which places recent MSU graduates in high schools as advisors throughout the state of Michigan.[35] She recalls that it was a lot of fun to represent MSU as an advisor, noting that the work she did helped several high school students find "any kind of college, two-year degrees or four, and even apprenticeships. I helped students with their applications and financial aid."[36] Her experiences with the MSU College Advising Corps rekindled an interest that was sparked during her time in the RCAH; Carrie soon found herself pursuing a graduate degree in student affairs with the plan of working in student life and affairs at a four-year university.

Carrie loved and eventually thrived in the small and inclusive environment that made up the RCAH. When she was a student in the residential college, she took several classes that impacted her professional development trajectory and current work style. She remembered, "When I first started in the RCAH, I was a student who needed a lot of help academically, and so I knew I needed some kind of something, I don't know like a mentor/mentee relationship, whether one-on-one or some kind of group."[37] She found a group of compatible people, or a network—professors, peers, and staff—who enabled her to accurately identify her needs, set goals, and then reach them while she was a student in the residential college.

Carrie remembers that several RCAH faculty and staff created comfortable, safe, and accessible spaces for students to learn and be challenged, and to express their personal and academic concerns and celebrations. She noted that these spaces would extend beyond a professor's office hours; these spaces were also classrooms, tutoring and learning centers, and spontaneous hallway conversations. The deliberate actions of RCAH faculty impacted Carrie's current job as a college advisor, so much so that she said,

When I have student come into my office, my immediate goal is to make them feel comfortable so that they'll want to come back. It's not my immediate goal to have them do the thing I need them to do. I want to meet them where they are figuratively and literally. And I learned to do all of this in the RCAH.[38]

Mentoring that is characterized by charitable and empathetic actions can result in positive and productive mentoring experiences. Carrie creates these comfortable and safe professional development experiences for her students because of her beliefs about how mentoring can factor into career-long learning.

Earlier in this chapter, Carrie indicated that she struggled during her first couple of years of college, both academically and professionally. Consequently, at the start of her senior year, Carrie found herself in "panic mode," as she described it, and in need of direction and guidance.[39] She knew what field she wanted to work in, but she was not sure how to apply to those kinds jobs or what to say and do during interviews. She recalled, "I took the career strategies course in RCAH. In the class, I had to do a job shadow, so I shadowed other people in student affairs."[40] Many of the assignments in the career strategies course were designed to help students locate their personal lives and goals in relation to their professional ones. Students were required to take the Myers–Briggs Type Indicator (MBTI), Strengths Finder assessment, and complete other small and large assignments such as drafting and revising resumes, cover letters, and going through mock interviews. Guest speakers rounded out the class, so that students could, according to Carrie, "hear from people in the area who do different things with their degrees and in their careers."[41] Of most significance to Carrie was a part of the career strategies course that may have seemed inconsequential to other students. She says,

In career strategies we would have a question of the day so that we could all learn about each other. I think when you do something like that with students, this little kind of exercise, makes you understand people and listen to other people, and helps you invest in someone else. This little exercise created other opportunities for more conversations.[42]

Listening to others, which is discussed in Chapter 3, enables a person to more clearly and accurately identify the networks, structures, disciplining mechanisms, and professional development that already exist in a company, organization, or even a classroom space. "These [networks] exist long before you enter a workspace," says Carrie, "and knowing this is hard to teach students. You have to be aware of your space, the importance of making things safe, and that these definitions will shift based on student."[43] In order to optimally grow professionally, a person must, as she continued, "get to know yourself, get to know other people, and then develop yourself professionally," and she furthers her story by adding that "the RCAH taught me to take a step back and see culture as it is," she stated, "and not necessarily as I want to see it or how I could change that culture."[44]

Carrie found herself in a different kind of mentoring relationship when she was a senior in college. This mentoring relationship was different from what she was previously used to—this time, Carrie would not be the mentee but the mentor. As a student in the RCAH, she was part of a co-ed a cappella group. The a cappella group performed around campus and at other East Lansing venues. As such, she was required to mentor a younger, novice singer in the group. Her experience mentoring the younger student, "taught me how to find balance in the relationship, to be friends, and to also figure out how to know when things are okay or not."[45] She noted, too, that flexible boundaries (but boundaries nonetheless) in the relationship were a must for her and the other student. The relationship she had with her peer influenced her approach to mentoring today. She says,

> it was important to keep boundaries. I mean, keeping doors open means that someone is going to come in, right? So being respectful of someone's time and energy, and being mindful of not being cruel. Like with my students now, I ask them, "Can we make an appointment and do this once a week?"[46]

The skills she learned in RCAH, Carrie believes, helps her set relationship boundaries in her current job with the students she advises. Keeping boundaries "open and dynamic" can be difficult to do, but it can greatly impact the productivity of the relationship.[47]

Case Example Three: Meet Samantha[48]

Samantha graduated in 2012 and was part of the second class to graduate from the residential college. A native of Michigan, Samantha knew that she wanted to attend college somewhere that was "not too big and not too small," particularly a university that would blend her love of art, music, culture, and community engagement.[49] But more importantly, she wanted to study at a university where she would be supported in big and small ways. These big and small ways can be linked to classroom and extracurricular learning moments, and also to the often-invisible work of professors advising students on which classes to take each semester. To illustrate, Samantha explained that a unique feature of the residential college was their approach to academic advising; students selected which professor they wanted as their advisor, as opposed to having an advisor selected for them. This practice alone, Samantha remembers, is a good example of how to "de-formalize the formal aspects of mentoring."[50] Advising and mentoring, she noted, are not the same, but one can beget the other; indeed, as this study has shown, mentoring happens in many and varied ways, and academic advising can be one way mentoring happens in a university setting.[51]

During her time in the RCAH, Samantha sought classes that covered topics related to campus and community engagement. She was someone who saw herself working for a nonprofit one day, and, as a result, took "the same kinds of classes with the same professors over and over again," because they aligned with her interests and passions.[52] And, like Alex and Carrie, Samantha knew she could reach out to RCAH faculty when she needed to, and could find support in the form of mentoring. The way she saw it, the relationships she cultivated with peers and faculty were just as impactful as the traditional book learning she was required to do. She remembered, "the professors in RCAH enjoy this [mentoring] aspect of their work, that they invite this kind of [mentoring] experience in."[53] To be sure, RCAH faculty did not only teach students specific content in history, literature, or the arts; faculty modeled relationship-building skills in their interactions with one another and with students. Samantha found the support she needed in RCAH, and she says that the kind of mentoring she received in the residential college "happened organically, but it happened for a reason."[54] All mentoring relationships begin with a purpose, she furthered, and her experiences with mentoring in the RCAH were no exception.[55]

After graduating from RCAH and MSU, Samantha took a job as a program coordinator for a mid-Michigan nonprofit organization. As a program coordinator, she occupied several different roles in education and outreach, and operational duties and special events. She also worked in fundraising and stewardship, focusing much of her time on working with new donors and patrons. When she started her job, however, she struggled to find her place in an existing network of relationships and work practices. She recalled, "I was trying to figure out what it means to do my job, and I realized it takes someone asking a question."[56] So, she reached out to her network of friends and colleagues and asked for advice on how to adjust to her new job. The advice she received was to keep her passion for music, art, and helping others at the center of every decision she made. Samantha said this advice helped her keep her job in perspective, adding that despite some ups and downs at work, she had never felt more empowered than when she stayed true to her personal convictions.[57]

Samantha approaches mentoring on a need-by-need basis. She says,

> I know if and when I need something. If I need something, and if whatever I'm currently doing isn't working for me, I know I need a change. So, I think of the people in my life and I email someone to see if they're available for coffee in the next two weeks or whatever.[58]

What is more, speaking about a recent professional development situation at her work, Samantha recalled, "once I invested in the city and the community around me, those people invested in me."[59] Reciprocal relationships, whether explicitly mentoring ones or not, can help foster a sense of belonging. And a sense of belonging or mattering is a "key moment in which people construct themselves or are constructed by others through relations with cultural forms in the arena of consumption."[60] Samantha never sacrificed her core beliefs and values, she did not conform to her workplace just because she felt a need to belong; instead she searched for common ground with her coworkers, and shared her differences and similarities with them, when appropriate.[61] Samantha's story illustrates that acceptance does not equal agreement, that investment does not mean enculturation.

Interestingly, Samantha identified an all-too-common assumption present in most mentoring relationships, stating "since women are supposed to be nurturing, or that's what we're supposed to believe, then mentoring should come naturally to us. We are expected to help other people."[62] Samantha corroborates Maria's views on gender and mentoring by pointing out that how a person is assumed or expected to mentor and be mentored is steeped in ideas about how one should perform their gender and sexuality. Investment mentoring can make these and other assumptions visible and can also provide mentors and mentees a way to address these assumptions and talk about expectations in mentoring and other workplace activities.

Investment mentoring can prepare students for their futures as knowledge workers, thought leaders, and experts in their fields. And as Samantha notes, this preparedness to be a productive member of society starts in the college classroom that is inclusive and fair.[63] Further, she believes that RCAH is becoming a good source of future leaders, leaders who are capable in their field of study as well as in their relationships with others. She feels that she was well prepared for her current work because, as she put it, the RCAH "gave me opportunities for real world application, so many opportunities to reach out to the community whether because of civic engagement courses or extracurricular community outreach."[64] She continued by adding, "RCAH classes were important, but finding others who could help me was even more important."[65] The ability to diversify her mentoring network has carried over to Samantha's current professional development style; she seeks out support from everyone in her life, regardless of background, education, or profession.

The mentoring stories RCAH alumni have contributed to this chapter are certainly meaningful. And their experiences of mentoring in the residential college and in different workplaces begin to shed light on the different ways mentoring happens throughout the course of a person's career. The mentoring experiences of HTI employees and RCAH alumni indicate that mentoring is not necessarily an organic process or set of practices that happens out of the blue as so many educators and industry professionals believe. Samantha noted that while the mentoring she experienced in the RCAH felt organic, she also commented on it having intentionality and purpose. What people experience as a natural coming together can be because of similar personalities, interests, and worldviews. While similar personalities or approaches to life can make mentoring easier or even more challenging, it remains clear that mentoring is situated, relational, and intentional.

Mentoring requires attentiveness, an honest interrogation and understanding of an individual's beliefs and core values, and a realistic plan of what a mentor and mentee hope to gain from the relationship. The stories from participants in this study show that investment mentoring in workplaces and classrooms can make moments of experiential learning more accessible, tangible, and valuable. This value-added approach to learning helps the participants in this study redefine success for themselves, while also offering up mentoring as a way to facilitate career-long, experiential learning from student, to employee, to administrator. If mentoring can help the participants in this study reconsider the importance of the kind of learning and professional development that enables them to learn over the duration of their career, then it can also help redefine the kinds of work that is valued in writing studies research, teaching, and service activities.

This chapter took a closer look at the invention and sustainability of mentoring in a particular university setting, the residential college in the arts and humanities at MSU. The ways in which mentoring happens in this unique school setting illustrates for rhetoric and writing teachers how mentoring that is learned and practiced in a school setting can help students transition to mentoring in non-school or work settings. In Chapters 4 and 5, the interviews with HTI participants suggested that non-academic, industry workers view mentoring as situated, personal, and relational. Further, HTI participants indicated that mentoring adheres to reciprocity, self-reflexivity (or self-awareness), and transparency. In this chapter, it is revealed that students can also experience mentoring in these ways. The connections among learning, mentoring in the classroom, and for career-long and workplace learning are now more visible and actionable.

This book focuses on mentoring that occurred in or because of traditional classroom spaces, alternative learning and living spaces (i.e., RCAH), as well as in non-academic workplace settings. Long-term pedagogical implications for writing studies certainly require collecting more and varied experiences of mentoring from different groups of people and in different learning spaces and workplaces. Still, RCAH participants supported what HTI participants noted as defining characteristics of positive mentoring: reciprocity, self-reflexivity (or self-awareness), and transparency. Moreover, RCAH participants identified three additional characteristics that mentors and mentees need for forming and sustaining positive mentoring relationships, both in school and work settings:

1. accountability and willingness,
2. relationship balance, and
3. flexible boundary setting.

First, RCAH participants indicated that for mentoring to be optimally productive, both mentor and mentee need to trust one another, talk with one another regularly, and try to help one another, especially during difficult or challenging times. In short, mutual accountability and willingness must be central to the relationship. Alex noted that he needs the option to invent mentoring that fits each set of circumstances he is in, and he can do this when he regularly communicates with his mentors. Mentoring for Alex is dependent on what he needs and when he needs it; his individual circumstances may change instantly, and knowing he has the support from someone he trusts can help him navigate both good and bad workplace situations.[66] The conditions that can affect mentoring range from specialized work projects and tasks to the geographical location and physical conditions (e.g., light, sound, temperature) of the space in which mentoring takes place. The available material and technological resources that can assist in mentoring someone also affect how the relationship is developed and maintained.

RCAH alumni agreed that a willingness to mentor or be mentored is also necessary. Willingness, they noted, is not to be confused with being assigned a mentoring relationship just for the sake of having one. While the practice of being formally assigned a mentor was infrequent in the residential college and was not done often by their current employers, RCAH alumni stated that being assigned a mentor would "feel forced" or "be pointless, especially if the mentor didn't know anything about [them] as a student or person."[67] Instead, RCAH alumni stated that the best kinds of mentoring they experienced in the college placed equal responsibility and accountability on both the mentor and mentee. Alex says that mentoring in

RCAH was most useful when it was "invent[ed] in whatever ways made sense to me and the other person involved."[68] Alex's mentoring experiences in this chapter revealed, similarly to Randall in Chapter 4, that mentoring is situated in context and time, and happens because of self-identified and mutual needs.

Second, similarly to HTI employees, RCAH participants indicated that mentoring happens in and because of a large system of professional development resources. The volume of these resources can, at times, be overwhelming, and so a person should seek out a balance of both formal and informal learning opportunities. Moreover, as Samantha noted, her network of professional development resources was made up of human and technological actors in the residential college, the larger MSU campus and surrounding East Lansing community, and other work and internship experiences both locally and globally.[69] Likewise, Carrie, put it well saying,

> Good mentoring doesn't necessarily mean happy or feel-good mentoring, but it does mean growth, learning something new, and awareness of self, of others, of privilege, and of your place in your community.[70]

Mentors and mentees must have an awareness of their individual and collective contributions to and expectations of the mentoring relationship. Carrie describes a kind of balance in being a mentor or a mentee. She understands herself as someone who is both separate from and connected to the mentoring relationship and other parts of her living and working environments.[71] Mentors and mentees are individuals in a community, acting in their environment, and contributing to it. Carrie's and Claire's mentoring experiences uphold the three investment mentoring criteria proposed earlier in this study as well as accountability and willingness, relationship balance, and flexible boundary setting proposed in this chapter to sustain positive and productive mentoring relationships.

And third, participants both at HTI and in the RCAH have shown that positive mentoring takes a lot of time and expends a lot of physical, mental, and emotional energy from both the mentor and mentee. The stories of both HealthTech and RCAH participants show that the physical, emotional, and intellectual labor of informal and formal mentoring can influence the ways in which mentoring relationships are formed, are sustained, and are mobilized from one work or class situation to another. To combat mentoring fatigue, mentors and mentees need to set firm but flexible borders around what the relationship is for—too many times, as Samantha commented, mentors and mentees can overextend themselves for the sake of the relationship.[72]

RCAH alumni suggested that one way to honor mentor and mentee willingness and accountability, relationship balance, and flexible boundary setting in the relationship is to practice these tactics in a low-stakes and safe learning environment like a classroom. Even though RCAH alumni did not experience explicit mentoring activities (i.e., learning how to be a mentor or mentee was not a class activity or graded assignment), they agreed that these kinds of exercises would have been a welcomed addition to their classes. These low-risk mentoring activities can help students practice how to mentor and be mentored, and also how to mentor in other school and professional spaces. Writing teachers are well positioned to help facilitate mentoring between students in the classroom because of small class sizes (which are similar to RCAH class sizes), and also the kinds of writing, reviewing, and revising activities that carry value in these spaces.

In the final chapter of this book, I sketch future research and pedagogical interventions emerging from this study. Of most significance to the final chapter of this study are the three, multi-step principles that can help rhetoric and writing teachers invent and facilitate mentoring in their classrooms and other learning spaces. These principles can help students and teachers become more transparent, self-reflexive (self-aware), and reciprocal mentors and mentees, which will help them throughout their careers.

Notes

1. Heather Noel Turner, Minh-Tam Nguyen, Beth Keller, Donnie Johnson Sackey, Jim Ridolfo, Stacey Pigg, Benjamin Lauren, Liza Potts, Bill Hart-Davidson, and Jeff Grabill, "WIDE Research Center as Incubator for Graduate Student Experience," *Journal of Technical Writing and Communication* 47, no. 2 (March 2017).
2. "Uniquely RCAH," Residential College in the Arts and Humanities, accessed May 20, 2018, http://rcah.msu.edu/about-rcah/uniquely-rcah.
3. "Graduate Fellows," Residential College in the Arts and Humanities, accessed May 20, 2018, http://rcah.msu.edu/about-rcah/uniquely-rcah.
4. Pseudonym used to protect identity.
5. Alex, in discussion with the author, March 2014.
6. Alex, interview.
7. Alex, interview.
8. "Professorial Assistantship," Michigan State University Honors College, accessed May 20, 2018, https://honorscollege.msu.edu/programs/professorial-assistantship.html.
9. Alex, interview.
10. Alex, interview.
11. Alex, interview.
12. Alex, interview.
13. Alex, interview.
14. Alex, interview.
15. Alex, interview.
16. Alex, interview.
17. Alex, interview.

18. Alex, interview.
19. Deborah Brandt, *Literacy in American Lives* (Cambridge: Cambridge University Press, 2001).
20. Alex, interview.
21. Alex, interview.
22. Alex, interview.
23. Alex, interview.
24. Alex, interview.
25. Alex, interview.
26. Alex, interview.
27. Alex, interview.
28. Alex, interview.
29. Alex, interview.
30. Brenton Faber, "Professional Identities: What Is Professional About Professional Communication?" *Journal of Business and Technical Communication* 16, no. 3 (July 2002).
31. Alex, interview.
32. The connections among dress, verbal expression, and mentoring appear to be many and are worthy of further study by rhetoric and writing practitioners.
33. Alex, interview.
34. Pseudonym used to protect identity.
35. "About MSU College Advising Corps," Michigan State University College Advising Corps, accessed May 20, 2018, www.collegeadvisingcorps.msu.edu/about.
36. Carrie, in discussion with the author, April 2014.
37. Carrie, interview.
38. Carrie, interview.
39. Carrie, interview.
40. Carrie, interview.
41. Carrie, interview.
42. Carrie, interview.
43. Carrie, interview.
44. Carrie, interview.
45. Carrie, interview.
46. Carrie, interview.
47. Jacqueline Jones Royster and Gesa Kirsch, *Feminist Rhetorical Practices: New Horizons for Rhetoric, Composition, and Literacy Studies* (Carbondale: SIU Press, 2012).
48. Pseudonym used to protect identity.
49. Samantha, in discussion with the author, April 2014.
50. Samantha, interview.
51. Samantha, interview.
52. Samantha, interview.
53. Samantha, interview.
54. Samantha, interview.
55. Samantha, interview.
56. Samantha, interview.
57. Samantha, interview.
58. Samantha, interview.
59. Samantha, interview.

60. Daniel Miller, "Why Some Things Matter," in *Material Cultures: Why Some Things Matter*, ed. Daniel Miller (London: UCL Press Limited, 1998), 9.
61. Samantha, interview.
62. Samantha, interview.
63. Samantha, interview.
64. Samantha, interview.
65. Samantha, interview.
66. Alex, interview.
67. Carrie, interview.
68. Alex, interview.
69. Samantha, interview.
70. Carrie, interview.
71. Carrie, interview.
72. Samantha, interview.

7 Using Investment Mentoring as a Framework for Seeing and Inventing Rhetorical Work

> I think of mentoring like this. Engage their heart. Engage their mind. And then get the hell out of the way. Because they'll be unstoppable.
>
> —Bill, HealthTech employee

In Chapter 2, I introduced a feminist, qualitative framework for examining professional identity development and experiential learning through an investment approach to mentoring. This framework was carried out by the HealthTech Industries (HealthTech or HTI) and Residential College in the Arts and Humanities (RCAH) participants' experiences of mentoring; from their stories, I showed how mentoring acts as a mode of experiential learning, as well as how a person's gender identity complicates and enriches how we understand mentoring. The experiences of mentoring from HTI and RCAH participants are more than just interesting to read. Their experiences predict possible other mentoring and professional development relationships and practices they will have over the duration of their careers.

In the fall of 2014, after the conclusion of this study, HealthTech had plans to begin to implement new practices at their Midwest location that would improve the performance and production of their goods and services. Change management—the collective term used to understand how organizations and companies prepare and support employees to successfully adopt change—helped HTI redefine job roles and titles, manufacturing workflow processes, and the kinds of and access to various technologies. These systematic changes in achieving company goals would affect the entire company at both individual and organizational levels. According to Chris, another senior-level employee at HTI, the need for efficient and inclusive change management practices at HealthTech became increasingly visible largely because of this study. These new workplace policies and practices, she happily reported, would consider all employees, from "production workers to executive-level management and other staff."[1]

Throughout the remainder of this chapter, I discuss some of the implications and recommendations of the feminist, qualitative framework developed and enacted in this book. Additionally, I offer some suggestions to
rhetoric and writing researchers and teachers that can help them facilitate
hands-on, practical learning and professional identity development with
their students and colleagues. To do this, the implications of an investment approach to mentoring are analyzed as is its impact on an individual's
career-long learning trajectory, specifically the experiences of mentoring
and other data collected from this study. These findings are important to
rhetoric and writing studies because they inform not only what can happen
inside the classroom, but also what can happen in different workplaces.
Next, I articulate how mentoring can be used as a rhetorical heuristic for
an individual's professional and personal identity development. Finally, I
briefly focus on future research and pedagogical interventions emerging
from this study. The findings from this study are examined alongside contemporary rhetoric and writing scholarship on the intersections of writing,
mentoring, and distributed cognition and knowledge work.[2]

Like others before me who have studied mentoring more generally and
mentoring in the workplace more specifically, HTI and RCAH participants' stories and experiences of mentoring could have been interpreted
as extensions or slight modifications of the hierarchical master/apprentice
models of mentoring that are commonly found in workplaces today.[3]
Instead, this study draws upon particular theories of feminism and individual and collective learning that allow for open and dynamic boundaries without sacrificing personal and professional efficacy. My overall
goal in working with the participants in this study was to locate, through
their experiences of mentoring, how investment mentoring practices get
invented in both school and non-school settings. My decision to prioritize
participants' experiences and stories of mentoring was simple; their experiences of mentoring seemed likely to produce a set of practices or guiding
principles that would help rhetoric and writing researchers and teachers
understand how mentoring can engage students to learn, think, and write
for their own definitions of success.[4] This study encouraged readers to shift
their thinking of mentoring as an object of study to a set of practices that
can be produced and reproduced in different contexts and institutions. It is
in this shift of *what* mentoring is to *how* it is invented and legitimized in
rhetoric and writing practice that this study and its proposed methodology
are most useful.

The methodology for this study can help teachers, researchers, and students
prioritize and participate in the retelling of their mentoring experiences,
rather than only report or assess the outcomes of each mentoring relationship or situation. What is more, this methodology held me accountable

to HTI and RCAH participants; not only was I able to share with them *my* professional and personal mentoring experiences, the methodology I assembled demanded it. The very actions that guided each of my inter-actions with participants were flexible, safe, and equitable. These actions allowed for participants to share their mentoring stories and experiences with one another as well as with me. As Chris commented during our final time together, "this interview was the most comfortable interviewing pro-cess I've ever been through . . . it didn't even feel like you were interview-ing me. It was so conversational." The investment mentoring characteristics I outlined in Chapter 2 were used in this study—I embodied reciprocity, self-awareness, and transparency with each participant in this study. My hope is that other writing studies teachers and researchers will use these characteristics in their teaching and research, and apply this methodology to the different kinds of projects they undertake.

With a different research site, or with a different grouping of employees from HealthTech or alumni from RCAH, this study could have focused more on how mentoring relationships facilitate other kinds of work or writ-ing and communication tasks. Instead, it focused on the ways individuals invent and invest in themselves and in one another. Through their stories and experiences of mentoring, which were as real time and down-to-earth as possible, I illustrated how their gender identities intersected with profes-sional development practices and their perceptions of those intersections of gender, work, and mentoring. Still, while the site is certainly impor-tant to the context of the study, the relationships and attitudes participants have toward investment mentoring matter the most in understanding how mentoring can facilitate other kinds of work and communication within their workplace.

Over the duration of this study, it has become clearer that this frame-work for understanding mentoring at HTI and RCAH is not only specific to HTI and RCAH and the employees and students who make up those spaces. Rather, this framework enables rhetoric and writing teachers and researchers to focus on how mentoring unfolds in local ways, ways respon-sive to the local conditions of their classrooms, research labs, programs, and departments. With this local understanding of how mentoring functions in a particular workplace, the definitions of success and what constitutes professional development can be rewritten in rhetoric and writing practice. Put another way, this study articulates how the invention of mentoring is connected to the larger ideological and socio-cultural commitments of each participant, and those commitments can dictate if and how mentoring is cre-ated in a given workplace. The stories and experiences participants shared in this study help to add to or challenge conceptions of how mentoring facilitates career-long, experiential learning.

Throughout this book, I position mentoring as a rhetorical heuristic for professional identity development, despite there being limitations to the study. This allowed me to begin to create a foundation for examining and developing sustainable writing curricula and writing programs that are centered on mentoring. Rhetoric and writing teachers and researchers certainly do use a variety of different and cutting-edge pedagogical and theoretical approaches to teaching and research that reflect what the discipline claims to value. To be sure, the practices and policies that inform rhetoric and writing programs, departments, and the field more generally often yield good results (i.e., graduates of these programs). And yet, while there is a healthy respect for mentoring in rhetoric and writing studies, there is nevertheless a limited perception of and appreciation for the transformative power mentoring has in shaping positive, long-term interactions with students and colleagues. The stories of Randall, Maria, Claire, and RCAH participants point to how mentoring affects their home lives and personal commitments to family, friends, and community, and even informs other daily work, writing, and communication tasks. Moreover, HTI participants commented repeatedly on how mentoring influences their relationships with one another at HTI and with their customers. In a similar way, how mentoring is invented and legitimized in rhetoric and writing practice must be reconceptualized, because mentoring is another pedagogical tool that can help students succeed in whatever they do. This study uncovers that an investment approach to mentoring is a more appropriate model of mentoring and instruction rather than one that promotes enculturation or conformity at the cost of creativity and learning.

Interestingly but not surprisingly, some participants' gender identities greatly affect their mentoring practices and their approaches to work. Several female participants noted that for them mentoring appears to be more high stakes than for their male coworkers. Participants talked extensively about their roles as spouses or partners, as caregivers to elderly parents, and as members of local and regional community organizations (e.g., local churches, and area 4-H clubs). Over and over again, HTI and RCAH participants emphasized how nearly impossible it was for them to separate certain parts of themselves and their lives from the work they do. The many personal and professional roles participants occupy indeed influence and tell how an individual develops as a professional. With their comments in mind, Donna Haraway's "Situated Knowledges: The Science Question in Feminism and the Privilege of Partial Perspective" is pertinent, especially when she writes,

> [Women] need an earth-wide network of connections, including the ability partially to translate knowledges among very different—and

power differentiated—communities. We need the power of modern critical theories of how meanings and bodies get made, not in order to deny meanings and bodies, but in order to live in meanings and bodies that have a chance for a future.[5]

For Maria and Claire especially, how they claim, express, and even compensate for their gender identities further complicate their access to and experiences of mentoring. Both Maria and Claire indicate there can be a great deal of privilege, often unearned, associated with gender identities that are considered more mainstream, normal, or typical. An investment approach to mentoring can welcome and celebrate diverse knowledges, positions, and identities, but it can be difficult to sustain if individuals refuse to consistently take responsibility for their worldviews and actions, and how those perceptions of reality affect the work they do and their relationships with coworkers.

Lucy Suchman's located accountability and Stacey Pigg's situated accounts of practice can help individuals take ownership for how their personal identifications affect their professional development and mentoring practices.[6] Situated accounts of work—work that is local, recognized as visible or invisible, and informs the production of texts and technologies—are available and valuable sites of rich interrogation and reinvention of what constitutes experiential and career-long learning.[7] These situated accounts of work must make connections across experiences, bodies, texts, and technologies that inform rhetorical, locatable, and critical knowledges. In Chapter 5, I illustrated the ways in which employees' situated experiences of mentoring are gendered. Therefore, Suchman's located accountability can now be expanded to include how various forms of visible and invisible work, such as the work of mentoring, are more all-or-nothing for some groups than they are for others.[8] The ability to locate oneself within a web of professional development should not be taken for granted; the time, resources, and physical and emotional energy it can take to do this locating is often a luxury that some cannot afford. Still, even small efforts, like engaging in an intentional hallway conversation with a colleague or taking the time to listen to them during a lunch break, can help a person be responsible for their participation in, sustainability of, or their undoing of such a web. Mentoring is, in fact, a real, bodily lived experience, an experience that has myriad outcomes that can be both good and bad.

Throughout this book, I have shown that investment mentoring experiences provide a useful through-point to understanding situated professional identity development for both rhetoric and writing studies as a discipline and as a way to teach those students. Pigg describes situated accounts of practice as "culturally situated, . . . detailed portraits of the work of rhetoric and writing" that can (and perhaps should) become the foundation of many kinds of discipline-specific action of contemporary rhetoric and writing teaching and research practice.[9] What is highlighted in this study, especially so, is that situated accounts of investment mentoring provide a way for rhetoric and writing practitioners to tackle the difficult questions surrounding what counts as success in the field's teaching, research, and service practices. Investment mentoring can open up spaces for productive dialogue about these very topics that undoubtedly affect student learning and professorial advancement and promotion in many writing and English departments.

Further, these situated accounts of investment mentoring within academic and non-academic workplace cultures present rhetoric and writing studies with explicit and visible moments to better value mentoring as a mode of career-long, experiential learning. The idea of building a mentoring network provides a useful frame to locate existing mentoring practices and invent new ones. For instance, when a mentoring network is constructed in a learning space (e.g., a classroom), moments of peer-to-peer learning can be easier to pinpoint, trace, and mobilize to other learning spaces and situations. Chapters 4 and 6 explained that mentoring happens in a variety of ways, and, although contextual, is not tied to one specific space or department at HTI or RCAH, and therefore could be transferred to other learning situations. Indeed, investment mentoring facilitates and promotes learning. In fact, its traceable quality is what makes its many performances quite unique, distinctive, and worthy of continued study by rhetoric and writing scholars.

Mentoring in academic and non-academic settings can reflect current understandings of what constitutes work, practice, relationship building, and success. The experiences of mentoring drawn upon in this study indicate similarly to Carol Berkenkotter, Thomas Huckin, and John Ackerman that moments of initiation into a specific discourse community manifest themselves in written text and also through interactions and relationships with peers and superiors.[10] When mentoring is understood as a self-directed or self-sought initiation and is actionable, then teachers and researchers can be more capable of locating and inventing moments of initiation in writing and mentoring alongside one another. In Chapter 6, participants illustrated that each writing act and mentoring experience can be lucid moments of identity building through which an individual not only learns the customs and conversations that would help them enter into desired professional communities, but also actively contributes to them and takes responsibility for those contributions. Investment mentoring can make visible and accessible the multiple languages, discourses, and other textual resources that sustain networked relationships for the employees at HTI, for RCAH alumni, and potentially for other kinds of professionals as well.

The feminist, qualitative framework on which this project is built enables writing studies scholars to continue the work of Goodburn, LeCourt, and Leverenz in redefining professional success in rhetoric and writing. Moments of "career training, knowledge-making, and disciplinarity," they write, work together to regulate the field through assumptions that manifest themselves in multiple ways.[11] This manifestation is clearest in how undergraduate majors and minors are constructed, how graduate student training and career advice is enacted, and how intradepartmental mentoring and other professional development practices are embraced or ignored. The lack of publicly visible demonstrations of success, or rather the lack of ranges of possible successes within rhetoric and writing studies, is indeed disheartening; however, a renewed understanding of mentoring, as I have showed in this book, can create room for richer and more contextualized approaches to informal and formal learning, which yield wider ranges of success for students and colleagues alike.

Rhetoricians building from this qualitative feminist framework for locating and inventing mentoring now have the opportunity to listen to other stories of mentoring, to collect and analyze artifacts associated with mentoring, and most importantly to continue building safety and value around the spaces and places, technologies, and bodies that support experiential learning in writing studies and beyond. Mentoring is not only inventive and rhetorical, but also multiple, situated, and always-already connected to gender identity. And it can help in revising current understandings and assumptions of what counts as success in rhetoric and writing studies.

Distributed Work and Institutional Critique: From Mentoring Relationships to Mentoring Networks

The mentoring experiences of HTI and RCAH participants shared in this study are intimately tied to knowledge work, distributed work, and institutional critique. As such, there are at least two areas for continued research emerging from this study. They are outlined below:

1. the distributed knowledge work practices of mentoring, and
2. the need for a mentoring-based institutional critique.

The macrostructures and microstructures by which mentoring, work, and gender are made visible converge with a range of contemporary rhetoric and writing studies research and scholarship. An investment approach to mentoring, with its fluid boundaries and dynamic interrelations, requires more complex understandings of mentoring, especially for and from marginalized groups who may not have access to or benefit from traditional, top-down mentoring relationships, alternative mentoring relationships, or even mentoring altogether. The networked model of investment mentoring outlined in this study can be a viable preference to traditional or customary ways of mentoring and career-long learning.

Networks of mentoring are one way to support knowledge creation in both academic and industry settings. Mentoring networks, according to Michelle Eble and Lynée Lewis Gaillet, enable individuals to see more clearly the distributed work of mentoring, work that can be challenging to manage because of its ethereal nature, and its multiplicity in workers, tasks, and distance.[12] This kind of work, Clay Spinuzzi writes, is "the coordinative work that enables sociotechnical networks to hold together and form dense interconnections among and across work activities that have traditionally been separated by temporal, spatial, or disciplinary boundaries."[13] Mentoring networks should rely on "negotiation, trust, alliances, agility, persuasion, and relationship building"; these networks are not constrained to space, place, or time.[14] Therefore, as Eble and Lewis Gaillet note,

> Focusing on these specific collaborative—and we argue, mentoring—skills helps highlight the possibilities inherent within a network that can lead to the synergistic and reciprocal relationships which constitute productive mentoring networks. These relationships, based on a network of people, disrupt the hierarchical nature of the traditional expert/protégé relationship that can be so exclusionary.[15]
>
> (p. 8)

Mentoring networks depend on multiple, culturally situated knowledges and resources, both human and technological alike. A distributed work understanding of mentoring allows for a more fluid transfer of knowledge throughout a person's network. A distributed work approach to mentoring can flatten and possibly disrupt hierarchies that are professionally exclusionary at best and personally destructive at worst.

The stories about and experiences of mentoring are abundant at Health-Tech and the RCAH at MSU. Participants used mentoring to interact with one another and other coworkers, and they also used mentoring to share information and knowledge about what happens in and because of their work environments.[16] Participants distribute knowledge to others in their network (and across other networks, too) and build supportive learning groups in their workplaces. Distributed networks can reinforce an investment approach to mentoring by making information immediate and accessible to all others in the network. With this new understanding of how mentoring can be invented, rhetoric and writing researchers and teachers (especially those who study and teach workplace, business, or technical communication and writing) have the opportunity to examine how individuals build relationships in their workplaces or departments that have a direct impact on their communication, writing, and long-term learning practices.

It can be common in writing studies teaching and research practices to separate writing from mentoring, or positioning writing as more important than mentoring. To clarify, rhetoric and writing teachers and researchers have not traditionally addressed mentoring as a set of rhetorical skills or practices that can help writers improve their writing, or help the field value research, teaching, and service equally. However, encouragingly, scholarship has been devoted to accounting for the ways in which intellectual and service work might be more equitably treated and rewarded in academic institutions.[17] This body of scholarship supports and informs this study by providing other ways of seeing mentoring as useful rhetorical work.

Institutional critique, according to James Porter, Patricia Sullivan, Jeffrey Grabill, Libby Miles, and Stuart Blythe is a "rhetorical practice mediating macro-level structures and micro-level actions rooted in a particular space and time," which moves beyond the classroom and the university.[18] The workplaces, departments, and institutions in which mentoring and learning takes place are "not monoliths; they are rhetorically constructed human designs (whose power is reinforced by buildings, laws, traditions, and knowledge-making practices) and so are changeable."[19] This type of macro and micro-level critique can, over time, produce rhetorical and material change by validating actions and practices that have long been discredited as "mere service work."[20] While service work is important to writing studies, investment mentoring can help reinterpret those often-discredited service actions and practices (like mentoring) as valuable extensions of intellectual and scholarly work. Mentoring is a micro-level action that makes visible how an institution is rhetorically constructed by human actions and interactions.

Mentoring, as I discussed in Chapter 2, is often positioned as an undervalued service to rhetoric and writing, and yet is done with more frequency, volume, and variety than teaching and research combined.[21] Mentoring can be viewed and used as a kind of mediated work that helps rhetoric and writing teachers and researchers interrogate their attitudes toward not only writing but also their allegiances to the larger, macro-level structures—the institutional and disciplinary networks—that contribute to what counts as knowledge creation, research, and teaching in the field of writing studies.

I also articulated in Chapter 2 that teaching and mentoring are complementary modes of learning. To reiterate, what this means is that teaching and mentoring can correspond to one another; they are two sides of the same coin. When students are active and positive peer mentors for one another, their opportunities for learning in the classroom and in other learning spaces increase. Positive peer-to-peer mentoring or peer investment mentoring can enable students to develop more critical rhetorical skills, reading and writing strategies, and beneficial relationships with one another. Again, this pedagogical shift in classroom writing and learning practices reflects contemporary writing studies and business communication scholarship about academic and workplace writing practices and strategies. Ultimately, peer-to-peer investment mentoring alongside writing instruction and peer review, provides rhetoric and writing teachers with a new way to teach students how to write and think critically about knowledge as a rhetorical production.

One way to teach mentoring in the writing classroom is by creating opportunities for students to learn how to be peer investment mentors and/or mentees. Rhetoric and writing teachers can develop peer mentoring activities alongside peer review activities in the classroom, and the following guiding principles can help them carry out such a task. The principles below, informed by HTI employee and RCAH alumni interviews, show how mentoring can be taught in writing classrooms alongside peer response or peer review. Teaching students to be reciprocal, reflexive, and transparent mentors and mentees is a pedagogical tactic that can inform rhetoric and writing teaching practices and curricula development. And it can, as Samantha noted, also better prepare students after graduation to be effective writers, communicators, and leaders in their new work environments.[22] Rhetoric and writing teachers can and should use mentoring as a pedagogical tool to teach students how to be responsible and effective peer reviewers. After all, writing well means investing in solid relationships with one another.[23]

Guiding Principles for Teaching Investment Mentoring in the Writing Classroom

Citing Janet Emig's groundbreaking study "Writing as a Mode of Learning," Beth Finch Hedengren writes in *A TA's Guide To Teaching Writing in All Disciplines* that the most successful writing "physically, visibly, and personally enhances students' learning."[24] Further, among the many characteristics Emig attributed to the idea of writing to learn, the characteristics of synthesis and analysis, active engagement with the material, and immediate and long-term feedback are most helpful when understanding the similarities between writing, peer review, and mentoring.[25] Drawing from Finch Hedengren's peer review strategies, I suggest three guidelines that can facilitate productive investment mentoring in classrooms and workplaces:

1. provide mentoring benchmarks,
2. plan or manage the mentoring process, and
3. hold one another accountable.

Coupled with the experiences and stories of mentoring from HTI and RCAH participants, the guidelines above can, in fact, help students become more reciprocal, self-reflexive (self-aware), and transparent mentors and mentees. The specific principles below are most effective when students of any grade level select their own mentoring relationship partners.

Principle One: Provide Mentoring Benchmarks

1. Acknowledge Power Differentials in the Relationship (Yes, These Do Exist)

There can be a tendency in some relationships for one person to take the lead over another. This person may be older, in a senior position, or have more professional experience than the other. The mentoring relationship is no different, and in fact imbalances of power can be quite common. Moreover, as Alex noted in Chapter 6, not addressing these differences in assumed or actual authority can leave one or more people in the relationship feeling used or misunderstood.[26] Have a conversation early in the relationship about status/rank, previous mentoring experiences, and the willingness to mentor or be mentored. Acknowledge that if a power dynamic is going to negatively impact the progress of the relationship, it might be a smart idea to find a new mentor or mentee.

2. Every Person Is a Work-in-Progress

Carrie demonstrates in Chapter 6 that, similarly to writing, every person is a work-in-progress.[27] Writing teachers often teach that writing is a process, and, as such, a student's draft can change in significant ways over the course of an assignment or semester. The same is true for how an individual develops professionally. If mentoring is approached in this way, then both mentor and mentee can discuss otherwise unrealistic expectations and inflexible practices, and leave those practices behind. Recognize the inclination to expect perfection in the relationship, and if possible, move beyond it.

3. Be Helpful and Also Challenging

Teachers often suggest that in peer review, students offer one piece of supportive feedback ("Your thesis statement is very clear. I understand what you will be arguing.") followed by a piece of feedback that is constructively critical or challenging ("I'm not sure what this evidence has to do with your topic sentence. How can you make your point clearer?"). Mentoring that offers both support and critique can help mentors and mentees pinpoint the value in the relationship and find new ways to address what is working and what is not. Suggest useful tactics for mentor/mentee improvement, but do not force or mandate such measures.

Principle Two: Plan and Manage the Mentoring Process or Relationship

1. Decide When and Where the Mentoring Will Take Place

To be most effective, mentoring can be planned in advance and with some measure of routine. Still, depending on the kind and type of mentoring that is sought (informal/formal), this step may prove to be more or less beneficial. Discussing when and where mentoring will happen, as Maria illustrated, can help both mentor and mentee think carefully about how to achieve the goals of the relationship.[28] The use of technological resources (e.g., Skype, WebEx, or other telecommunication application) can also help facilitate mentoring conversations if face-to-face interaction is not possible or preferred.

2. Collaborate on Learning Goals and Relationship Outcomes

Mentoring is most generative when mentor/mentee learning goals and outcomes are mutual and reciprocal. To achieve optimum benefit, the mentor and mentee should work together when planning the relationship's "roadmap." This means that when deciding the goals of the relationship, both the mentor and mentee should contribute to the formation and development of the goals. Further, collaboration can ensure that both mentor and mentee are responsible for the learning that happens as a result of the mentoring.

Principle Three: Hold One Another Accountable

1. Encourage Status Reports or Progress Updates

Mentors and mentees should regularly check in with one another. As was stated earlier in this chapter and the introduction, using technological platforms that facilitate voice and video communication (e.g., Skype, WebEx, or other platform) can provide mentors and mentees with a fast, reliable, and easy-to-use application to update one another on the progress of a task or activity. Additionally, making a phone call, or sending an email or text message can also clarify any uncertainty or confusion in the relationship. And certainly, celebratory updates can provide mentors and mentees with a sense of satisfaction and connection. Simply put, when mentors and mentees check in with one another, they are actively investing in the life of the mentoring relationship.

2. Build In Rewards and Celebrations

When a learning goal or professional outcome is achieved, big or small, it should be recognized with an appropriate celebration. Send the mentor or mentee an electronic (email) or handwritten paper card, or go out for coffee or lunch. Whatever reward is decided, make sure that the appreciation behind it is visible and genuine.

3. Do Not Be Afraid to Assess the Relationship and Move On If Necessary

Not all relationships are meant to last a lifetime, and mentoring ones are no exception. Some mentoring relationships end because all of the learning tasks and goals have been successfully completed and attained. When this happens, it is a good time to assess the relationship and decide whether it should continue. Often, but not always, mentors and mentees agree to remain friendly and collegial with one another, and keep the door open should any other development opportunity arise.[29] Still, some mentoring relationships diminish over time because of the attitude, actions, or lack of interest of either the mentor or mentee. Tensions and difficulties can crop up in the mentoring relationship, and sometimes these tensions can lead to growth for the mentor, mentee, or both.[30] If either the mentor or mentee feel misunderstood, taken advantage of, or physically and/or emotionally unsafe, then the relationship should end, and any necessary disciplinary actions should be taken. Since the mentor and mentee are assumed to be capable agents of their own learning, mutual agreement from the mentor and mentee is not needed to end the relationship.

I have illustrated throughout this book that rhetoric and writing researchers and teachers should consider or reconsider the rhetorical and relational habits created and used as writing, researching, and learning pedagogies. As the courses taught in university classrooms expand from first-year and second-year writing, technical report writing and business and administrative writing, to courses in usability research, user-centered design, and experience architecture, implementing peer investment mentoring in writing classrooms can help students understand that writing well can come from investing in constructive and critical relationships with one another. Therefore, the more opportunities students have to practice modeling and building positive investment mentoring relationships with one another, the better chance they have of employing reciprocal, self-reflexive (or self-aware), and transparent writing and communication strategies when working with and for local and global citizens and enterprises. Investment mentoring is best understood as a complex weaving of stories, histories, vulnerability, and trust.[31] The implications mentoring has on professional identity development directly impact the scholarship, teaching, and service requirements in rhetoric and writing studies. To continue to build value in rhetoric and writing practice, teachers and researchers must evaluate their commitments to ideologies, theories, pedagogies, and stories that either produce or impede generative, sustainable relationship-building practices.

Rhetorical Strategies for Professional Development: Investment Mentoring in Classrooms and Workplaces is a place to start, a way to visibly call attention to how mentoring and learning are valued in non-academic workplace settings, in rhetoric and writing studies broadly, and how writing programs can contribute to workplace learning beyond the classroom. In turn, future research must take up the shortcomings of this study with the goal of creating attentive and nuanced understandings of the role mentoring plays in writing and learning. There is certainly more work to be done in locating, uncovering, and challenging the stories of colleagues (both in academia and industry), of students, and others who have taken alternative routes for their careers. The more and varied accounts of mentoring that are recorded and collected from our discipline, the more teachers and researchers can be accountable to and participate in expanding the dominant definitions of what counts as professional success in the field of rhetoric and writing studies.

Notes

1. Chris, in discussion with the author, June 2014.
2. Dorothy Winsor, *Writing Power: Communication in an Engineering Center* (Albany: SUNY Press, 2003); Peter Morville, *Ambient Findability* (Sebastopol: O'Reilly, 2005); William Hart-Davidson, Clay Spinuzzi, and Mark Zachary, "Visualizing Writing Activity as Knowledge Work," *Proceedings of the 24th Annual International Conference on Design of Communication* (Myrtle Beach, SC, 2006); Michelle F. Eble and Lynée Lewis Gaillet, *Stories of Mentoring: Theory and Praxis* (West Lafayette: Parlor Press, 2008); Jason Swarts, *Together With Technology: Writing Review, Enculturation and Technological Mediation* (Amityville: Baywood, 2008); Liza Potts, "Using Actor Network Theory to Trace and Improve Multimodal Communication Design," *Technical Communication Quarterly* 18, no. 3 (2009); William Hart-Davidson and Jeffrey Grabill, "Understanding and Supporting Knowledge Work in Schools, Workplaces, and Public Life," in *Writing in Knowledge Societies*, eds. Doreen Starke-Meyerring, Anthony Paré, Natasha Artemeva, Miriam Horne, and Larissa Yousoubova (Fort Collins: WAC Clearinghouse, 2011).
3. Kathy Kram and Lynn Isabella, "Mentoring Alternatives: The Role of Peer Relationships in Career Development," *Academy of Management Journal* 28 (1985); David Clutterbuck, *Everyone Needs a Mentor: Fostering Talent in*

Your Organization (Wimbledon: CIPD,1985); Victoria Showunmi, "A Black Perspective on Mentoring," *Mentoring & Tutoring: Partnership in Learning* 3, no. 3 (1996).

4. These guiding principles are discussed later in this chapter.

5. Donna Haraway, "Situated Knowledges: The Science Question in Feminism and the Privilege of Partial Perspective," *Feminist Studies* 14, no. 3 (1988): 187.

6. Lucy Suchman, "Working Relations of Technology Production and Use," *Journal of Computer-Supported Cooperative Work* 2 (1994); Lucy Suchman, "Located Accountabilities in Technology Production," *Scandinavian Journal of Information Systems* 14, no. 2 (2002); Stacey Pigg, "Embodied Rhetoric in Scenes of Production: The Case of the Coffeehouse" (Doctoral Dissertation, Michigan State University, 2011).

7. Pigg, "Embodied."

8. Suchman, "Located."

9. Pigg, "Embodied."

10. Carol Berkenkotter, Thomas N. Huckin, and John Ackerman, "Conventions, Conversations, and the Writer: Case Study of a Student in a Rhetoric Ph.D. Program," *Research in the Teaching of English* 22, no. 1 (1988): 193.

11. Amy Goodburn, Donna LeCourt, and Carrie Leverenz, "Introduction," in *Rewriting Success in Rhetoric and Composition Careers*, eds. Amy Goodburn, Donna LeCourt, and Carrie Leverenz (Anderson: Parlor Press, 2013), x.

12. Michelle Eble and Lynee Lewis Gaillet, "Re-inscribing Mentoring," in *Realizing the Dream: Essays in Pursuit of a Feminist Rhetoric*, eds. Jessica Enoch and Jordynn Jack (forthcoming).

13. Clay Spinuzzi, "Guest Editor's Introduction: Technical Communication in the Age of Distributed Work," *Technical Communication Quarterly* 16, no. 3 (2007): 268.

14. Spinuzzi, "Guest," 271–272.

15. Eble and Lewis Gaillet, "Re-inscribing," 8.

16. Peter Morville, *Ambient Findability* (Sebastopol: O'Reilly, 2005).

17. Goodburn, LeCourt, and Leverenz, *Rewriting*; Kendall Leon and Stacey Pigg, "Graduate Students Professionalizing in Digital Time/Space: A View From 'Down Below'," *Computers and Composition* 28 (2011); Gail Y. Okawa, "Diving for Pearls: Mentoring as Cultural and Activist Practice among Academics of Color," *College Composition and Communication* 53, no. 3 (February 2002).

18. James E. Porter, Patricia Sullivan, Jeffrey Grabill, Libby Miles, and Stuart Blythe, "Institutional Critique: A Rhetorical Methodology for Change," *College Composition and Communication* 51, no. 4 (2000): 612.

19. Porter, Sullivan, Grabill, Miles, and Blythe, "Institutional," 611.

20. Porter, Sullivan, Grabill, Miles, and Blythe, "Institutional," 627, 631–632.

21. Theresa Enos, *Gender Roles and Faculty Lives in Rhetoric and Composition* (Carbondale: SIU Press, 1996); Rebecca Rickly and Susanmarie Harrington, "Feminist Approaches to Mentoring Teaching Assistants: Conflict, Power, and Collaboration," in *Preparing College Teachers of Writing: Histories, Theories, Programs, and Practices*, eds. Betty Pytlik and Sarah Liggett (New York: Oxford University Press, 2002); Sally Barr Ebest, "Mentoring: Past, Present, and Future," in *Preparing College Teachers of Writing: Histories, Theories, Programs, and Practices*, eds. Betty Pytlik and Sarah Liggett (New York: Oxford University Press, 2002); Pamela VanHaitsma and Steph Ceraso, "'Making It' in the Academy Through Horizontal Mentoring," *Peitho* 19, no. 2 (2017).

22. Samantha, in discussion with the author, April 2014.
23. These guiding principles can also be used between and among faculty in writing programs and English departments. For the sake of this chapter, I am focusing on student mentoring in the classroom.
24. Janet Emig, "Writing as a Mode of Learning," *College Composition and Communication* 28, no. 2 (May 1977); Beth Finch Hedengren, *A TA's Guide to Teaching Writing in All Disciplines* (New York: Bedford/St. Martin's, 2004).
25. Emig, "Writing," 123–124, 128.
26. Alex, in discussion with the author, March 2014.
27. Carrie, in discussion with the author, April 2014.
28. Maria, in discussion with the author, February 2014.
29. Randall, in discussion with the author, February 2014.
30. Maria, interview; Claire, in discussion with the author, February 2014.
31. Alex, interview.

Index

Printed in the United States
by Baker & Taylor Publisher Services